# BITCOIN PRENEUR

## A BEGINNERS GUIDE TO BITCOIN, AND EVERYTHING YOU NEED TO KNOW TO START INVESTING

ABDUL VASI

# TABLE OF CONTENTS

| | |
|---|---|
| WHY I WROTE THIS BOOK | i |
| 3 WAYS TO GET THE MOST OUT OF THIS BOOK | iv |
| **1-BITCOIN: AN INTRODUCTION TO DIGITAL MONEY** | **5** |
| 1.1. BITCOIN: WHAT IS THE FUSS ALL ABOUT? | 6 |
| 1.2. DOES IT RUN OR FLY? HOW DOES BITCOIN WORK? | 8 |
| 1.3. A LITTLE SNEAK PEEK AT USING BITCOIN | 10 |
| **2 - EVOLUTION OF MONEY: THE ROAD TO BITCOIN** | **13** |
| 2.1. HISTORY OF HUMAN MONETARY SYSTEM: THE EVOLUTION STORY | 15 |
| 2.1.1. The Beginning of Money — The Road to Coins | 16 |
| 2.1.2. A Bizarre Invention - The Paper Money | 17 |
| 2.1.3. The Invention of Plastic Money: The Game of Cards | 18 |
| 2.1.4. Bitcoin: A new beginning? | 19 |
| **3 - SECURITY, STRENGTH, IDENTITY OR SURVEILLANCE? REASONS BEHIND THE RISE OF BITCOIN** | **21** |
| 3.1. THE REDUNDANT BANKING SYSTEM: A GRAVE TRANSFORMATION OF A GREAT CREATION | 22 |
| 3.2. NARROWING CIRCLE: REDUCED ACCESS TO THE BANKING SYSTEM | 23 |
| 3.3. BITCOIN AND THE HOPE FOR BETTERMENT | 25 |
| 3.4. THE CALL FOR A NEUTRAL SYSTEM | 26 |
| 3.5. DECENTRALISING MONEY | 27 |
| 3.6. A CURRENCY FOR THE FUTURE | 28 |
| **4 - PRINCIPLES OF BITCOIN DESIGN** | **31** |
| 4.1. BITCOIN ARCHITECTURE: TIMESTAMP SERVER AND TRANSACTIONS | 32 |
| 4.1.1. Understanding Transactions in Bitcoin | 33 |
| 4.1.2. Function of Timestamp Server | 35 |
| 4.1.3. Comprehending The Bitcoin Network | 36 |
| 4.2. BLOCKCHAIN TECHNOLOGY: EVERYTHING YOU NEED TO KNOW | 37 |

## 5 - AN INTRODUCTION TO THE WALLETS AND THE COINS: GETTING STARTED WITH BITCOIN — 41
5.1. WHAT ARE BITCOIN WALLETS? — 42
    5.1.1. Hardware wallets — 43
    5.1.2. Paper wallets — 44
    5.1.3. Web-based wallets — 46
    5.1.4. Software wallet — 47
5.2. HOW TO BUY BITCOINS? — 47

## 6 - INVESTING IN BITCOIN: THE GOOD, THE BAD AND EVERYTHING YOU SHOULD KNOW — 49
6.1. THE ADVANTAGES AND DISADVANTAGES OF BITCOIN INVESTMENT — 50
    6.1.1. The Advantages of Investing in Bitcoin — 50
    6.1.2. Disadvantages of investing in Bitcoin — 52
    6.1.3. Should you invest in Bitcoin? — 53
6.2. THE STRATEGY OF MAKING BITCOIN INVESTMENT — 54
    6.2.1. What should you know to invest money? — 55
6.3. IMPORTANT SUGGESTIONS FOR MAKING BITCOIN INVESTMENT — 56

## 7 - THE CURRENT PAIN OF MONEY TRANSFER AND BANK A/Cs — 59
7.1. WHY THE MODERN DAY BANKING SYSTEM HAS BECOME PAINFUL? — 60
7.2. IS BITCOIN THE ANSWER TO TODAY'S BANKING PROBLEMS? — 62
7.3. LEGAL OR ILLEGAL: THE VERDICT ON BITCOIN — 65

## 8 - BITCOIN: IS IT A THREAT OR A GIFT? — 67
8.1. THE SKEPTICISM AROUND BITCOIN: A HISTORICAL APPROACH — 68
8.2. IS IT POSSIBLE TO COMPREHEND BITCOIN'S FULL ABILITIES? — 70
8.3. IS BITCOIN REALLY A CURSE FOR THE MODERN WORLD? — 72

## 9 - BITCOIN VS. ALTCOINS — 75
9.1. ALTCOINS: THE ALTERNATIVE CRYPTO-CURRENCIES — 76
    9.1.1. Popular Altcoins: Cryptocurrencies that show a lot of promise — 77
    9.1.2. Ethereum — 78

| | |
|---|---|
| 9.1.3. Litecoin | 79 |
| 9.1.4. Lisk | 79 |
| 9.2. BITCOIN OR ALTCOINS: THE BEST PLACE FOR INVESTING | 80 |
| **10 - EXTRAORDINARY ALTCOINS – TAKING AHEAD THE LEGACY OF BITCOINS** | **85** |
| 10.1. IOTA | 86 |
| 10.2. NEO | 88 |
| 10.3. MONERO | 89 |
| 10.4. CARDANO (ADA) | 90 |
| 10.5. GROESTLCOIN | 91 |
| 10.6. VERTCOIN | 92 |
| 10.7. DASH | 93 |
| **FAQs ON BITCOIN** | **97** |
| **CRYPTO TRADING & INVESTING LESSONS LEARNED OVER THE PAST YEARS** | **127** |
| **CRYPTOCURRENCY EXCHANGES IN INDIA** | **133** |
| **ABOUT OUR SERVICES** | **134** |

# WHY I WROTE THIS BOOK

Investing money is easily done; however, earning profits and success from your investments is really hard to achieve.

"Do not run behind success, it will do you no good." This is something that we often hear. But is it true in real life? No! If you truly hate to fail, only then can you achieve success. If you are an investor, you must remember this always.

I wrote this book to introduce you to Bitcoin, which in my opinion is a marvelous invention. It is my hope that, with every chapter of this book, you will develop more interest in Bitcoin and get th e urge to get started with it. So, this is the right time for me to share with you the reason why I wrote this book.

Being an entrepreneur for almost 17 years, I have learned a great deal about success and failures. Success is something that is really hard to achieve unless you have something or someone to guide you down the right path.

How do I know it? I failed in hundreds of things before achieving the success that I have today. But I never gave up during all those troubled times. I kept my mind focused and prepared myself to achieve.

The thing you need to understand is that success and failure are two sides of the same coin. It is normal for everyone to experience both in life. However, you cannot let that leave a permanent mark on your life. You need to keep hating failure and strive hard to achieve success.

## WHY I WROTE THIS BOOK

Still, it is time-consuming. I have spent 17 years failing then rising from the ashes. But when it comes to Bitcoin, there is no need for you to spend so much time in this loop. If you are becoming a Bitcoinpreneur then your journey will always be to the land of success.

Actually, that's the reason behind writing the book. I want to help you achieve success with my experience and knowledge as documented in the pages of this book. There is no need for you to make the mistakes that I have made.

I actually did not know much about Bitcoin even months before writing this book. I knew that it was a cryptocurrency and some people were excited about it. But I had no clear sense of this breathtaking technology. Luckily, a friend introduced to me to Bitcoin and I was immediately enthralled by it.

Since then I have spent hours and days researching Bitcoin and Altcoins, investing money and getting excited about the extraordinary changes that these cryptocurrencies are bringing to our payment and banking system.

During this time, that's when it really hit me. I realized that I could share the knowledge that I obtained with you, thereby sparing you all the hours of research and headache. Since I like to call this book an accessible guide, you will start understanding the concept behind Bitcoin and Altcoins as you turn the pages.

To be honest, my actual interest in Bitcoin started after I read **The Internet of Money** by Andreas Antonopoulos. Actually, his work was one of my major inspirations for writing this book in order to transmit the knowledge that I have gained to you.

As a matter of fact, I had been working a book about effective employee management, but I delayed that to devote myself completely to developing this book about Bitcoin as the technology is truly fascinating.

## WHY I WROTE THIS BOOK

There are a few people that I need to thank for helping me make this book a reality. I need to thank my co-writer Ankita Roy Choudhury for working with me and giving a proper shape to the book, as well my copy editor Marcia Abramson. I also need to thank my friend Mayur Saparia for introducing me to this incredible technology.

Finally, I need to thank my beautiful wife and three lovely daughters for supporting me through everything and providing me with the courage to make this book happen.

As leadership expert Robin Sharma has said, "Remember that to double your income, triple your investment in learning, coaching and self-education."

And this is a book to triple your investment.

**But remember: This is not a get-rich-quick book. It is to help you understand the concept of Bitcoin. So, do your research before investing as I will not be responsible for your losses. Invest as per your risk appetite since that is the key to winning.**

# 3 WAYS TO GET THE MOST OUT OF THIS BOOK

**1. Agree to disagree** – You will not agree with all the content the first time you read it. That's okay. We all have our own opinions and you may see something in a way which I never could. That is what makes us individuals. So, you don't need to agree with me on everything. Read the book anyway. Why am I saying that? Well, it will help you to form your own opinions. Keep reading and keep disagreeing to shape up your individual views.

**2. Stop frequently in your reading to think about what you are reading** – Our mind and intellect are the greatest gifts that we have. I want you to make good use of them while reading this book. There is nothing to rush about. Take a pause and think about what you have just read. It will help you to better understand the beautiful technology of Bitcoin and to formulate your own Bitcoin strategies. A Bitcoinpreneur can be anyone. All you have to do is to read the book, think and improvise!

**3. Skip around to maintain your interest** – If there is any chapter that you wish to read later, you are free to do so. There is nothing wrong with it. Get on the chapters that interest you most and finish them first. Once you have done that, you can finish the leftover chapters easily with peace of mind.

So, what are you waiting for? It is time to get started with Bitcoin!

## CHAPTER ONE

# BITCOIN: AN INTRODUCTION TO DIGITAL MONEY

Cryptocurrency has become the talk of the town these days. You probably have heard about it by now. And not just cryptocurrency, but specifically Bitcoin, which has given a new meaning to the word cryptocurrency. Though it was not the first, it has been the most significant one since its inception back in 2008.

### But what is Bitcoin?

It has been in the news and social media for quite a long time. Everyday people, celebrities, monetary experts, everyone is expressing their excitement about it. That's because it is the next step for human civilization towards a better future. Bitcoin is the future!

### What is the most interesting invention that computer science has made in the last two decades?

You will probably think about laptops, the high-tech hardware, and microchips that are available in the market. But the answer to the question is Bitcoin!

Bitcoin has been simply termed as "digital money." It's not entirely true. It is an oversimplification. Like the internet is not just Google, Bitcoin is not just digital money.

**Bitcoin is an international payment system, a currency, a great place to invest and above all it is a highly advanced technology. Some of the experts also call it a cryptocurrency.**

However, the best thing about Bitcoin is that it's not centralized. Moreover, it does not rely on any bank or financial institution. Plus, there is no governmental control over it. It is unique by its own rights.

Bitcoin is not just a fascinating invention in computer science in the last two decades. Bitcoin is so much more than that. It is the change that is most necessary for the socio-economic system of today. So, let's get started with unveiling the mysteries of Bitcoin.

## 1.1. BITCOIN: WHAT IS THE FUSS ALL ABOUT?

As I said before, Bitcoin can be simply described as digital money or digital currency. It's true that Bitcoin is like the dollar or pound. It is obviously a valid currency. But there is one big difference! It is not owned or monitored by any government on earth. It is completely decentralized.

You can use Bitcoin like any normal currency. You can buy things, you can save money in your Bitcoin account and you can even transfer money to someone with the help of Bitcoin. Perhaps the best thing about Bitcoin is that you can transfer money anywhere in the world by paying a minimal transaction fee.

Yes, you will have to pay a fee but one that is much less than the rates charged by the banks and centralized financial institutions. This is one of the reasons that I choose to call Bitcoin "the future of money." And I assure you there is much more to it!

## Is Bitcoin an invention?

The answer is simple! Bitcoin came into being as a technological invention. Back in 2008, a person using the pseudonym Satoshi Nakamoto first informed the world that it is possible to build a blockchain network like Bitcoin. In the paper he published, he showed that it is plausible to create a decentralized network that can work perfectly without any controlling authority. (If the concept of the blockchain is new to you, see section 4.2 for a basic introduction.)

Though there were criticisms at the time and some even called Nakamoto's claim fake, within three months of the publication of his paper he created a software which shut up his critics. That software was the key to building the network that Bitcoin uses today. So, when I called it the fascinating invention in the last 20 years in computer science, I wasn't overexaggerating.

But Bitcoin is not a company like PayPal, Visa or MasterCard. Neither is it an online application of some sort. It is better to call Bitcoin a protocol. It is similar to the IP address that you use.

Bitcoin works on some simple mathematical rules to which everyone using it agrees.

Hence, it cuts the need for a centralized body.

Of course, Bitcoin is a currency too like the US dollar or Indian rupee. The only difference is that it is not under the control of any government. It is necessary to understand that currency is just an application of Bitcoin. The invention itself has much more to it than it meets the eye.

I came across Bitcoin back in May 2017 and it immediately caught my attention. I really felt like I was hitting a jackpot since the possibilities that I saw in this program were boundless. I have been familiar with the internet since it was introduced in my country of India and I cannot recall having ever seen anything which had me completely overwhelmed like Bitcoin. I could feel that it was the key to improve our failing monetary system.

Since we live in the world of social media, it is unlikely that you have not heard of Bitcoin. You may have heard that it is a currency, a great payment system or something entirely different. I ask you to forget all of that!

Respect and embrace Bitcoin as a technology. You do not need to remember that it is a great currency or that it lets you transfer money at zero or minimal fees. These are not important. These do not make Bitcoin special; what makes it special is the innovative technology behind it and the endless possibilities that it offers.

## 1.2. DOES IT RUN OR FLY? HOW DOES BITCOIN WORK?

As I have said before, Bitcoin works on some simple mathematical rules. Everyone transacting money through Bitcoin agrees to these rules which remove the need for any centralized network.

**But how does it work? How will you get started with Bitcoin?**

These are some general questions that are bound to come to your mind. Let me make the answers clear to you!

You are likely familiar with online wallets and how they work. The working of Bitcoin is kind of similar to those wallets.

To get started with Bitcoin, you first have to get a Bitcoin wallet. Yes, it is similar to opening a bank account. There are several types of wallets available in Bitcoin and you can easily choose the one that fits you best. But that is a topic for another chapter; so let me keep that for the future. As I said, the process is really very simple. Get your Bitcoin wallet, buy Bitcoins from Bitcoin exchanges and that's all you need to do to participate in this extraordinary technology.

From this point, it becomes completely different than anything you have used before. Once you transfer the funding to your account, it gets converted to the digital currency or Bitcoins. That is all you need to do to start your own Bitcoin account. Interestingly, you can transfer the fund or Bitcoins to any other Bitcoin account in any part of the world instantaneously.

## How does this transaction work?

This is the second biggest question that comes to mind after how to get started with Bitcoin.

I have previously told you that Bitcoin runs on a blockchain network. The term blockchain is the key to understanding the complex mathematical process behind the working of Bitcoin.

Blockchain can be viewed as the digital version of the ledgers that banks use to record the transactions between accounts. So, it is basically a public digital ledger!

When you enter the amount and hit the transfer button on your Bitcoin account, your Bitcoin wallet provides the blockchain network with a mathematical proof to ensure that a transaction is being made.

The mathematical proof is provided with the help of the cryptographic signature that your Bitcoin wallet uses. Once the transaction is complete it becomes a block and is added to the blockchain like a link in an actual chain.

That's how the transaction of money works!

However, you will never have to worry about anything. Making a transaction with Bitcoin is much like sending an email. Just add the amount and hit the send button, the work will be done instantly. There is no need for any authority or centralization. After every ten minutes, the decentralized blockchain network updates itself and agrees on the transactions that have been made.

Most of us do not know the complex technological functions behind an email; similarly, it is not important for you to know in detail the complicated mathematical problems that are associated with Bitcoin.

## So, what is the point of telling you the working of Bitcoin?

Well, it is to help you understand the technology behind Bitcoin.

## 1.3.A LITTLE SNEAK PEEK AT USING BITCOIN

### How can you use Bitcoin?

I guess you can answer this question pretty well now!

I have already told you that Bitcoin has the ability to operate as a separate currency. So, you can easily use Bitcoin to buy anything. In other words, it can be used as normal currency.

But there is something that Bitcoin offers which normal currencies do not. The currencies like the dollar, euro and Indian rupee are all controlled by their respective governments. So, you cannot use them in any other country. On the contrary, Bitcoin is not operated by any government since it is completely decentralized. Hence, it is accepted worldwide. No matter where you are in the world, if you have an internet connection, you will be able to get what you need using Bitcoin.

I am an entrepreneur and so are many of you. Our main motive is to sell our products to our customers and in return accept payments. The biggest problem in setting up a global business today is accepting payment. There is no denying that there are several apps that allow you to accept online payments internationally. But they deduct a good amount of money to cover various charges.

Well, Bitcoin is the savior. It can help you to get rid of such problems. As I have said before, Bitcoin uses a decentralized blockchain network. So, there is no question of a centralized body controlling the whole payment system. It means the Bitcoin network does not require any authorization from a centralized body, rather it uses a few mathematical equations to run.

Secondly, the blockchain ledger cannot be altered by anyone even though it is public. Thus, there is no chance of any third party imposing any kind of tax or charge on the money you receive. This emphasizes another exciting feature of Bitcoin. As I said, it is virtually impossible to tamper with the blockchain ledger. As a result, Bitcoin offers you utmost security.

"When I first heard about Bitcoin, I thought it was impossible. How can you have a purely digital currency? Can't I just copy your hard drive and have your bitcoins? I didn't understand how that could be done, and then I looked into it and it was brilliant." -Jeff Garzik, CEO of Bloq Inc.

**CHAPTER TWO**

# EVOLUTION OF MONEY: THE ROAD TO BITCOIN

### How different is Bitcoin from the normal money?
### Why is Bitcoin so important?

People always ask me such questions. However, it is not possible to answer them without talking about the history of money. So, let me provide you with a historical context of money so you can understand the importance of Bitcoin in this context.

### Understanding the real age of money:

Before we get started, I have a little question for you. Here goes:

**How old do you think money is? If you consider money as a form of technology which any ancient civilization had created, then how old would that be?**

**Is money 2,000 years old? 10,000 years old?**

A plethora of numbers may be circulating in your mind. However, the truth is that we do not know yet. It is yet to be discovered how old money actually is. Why am I saying that it is yet to be discovered? It is because we have not yet discovered any civilization so old that it predates money.

Till now all the civilizations that we have discovered had money in some form. Be it the barter system or clay tablets, even in the most ancient civilizations like the Harappan or the Mesopotamian, money was present.

## Feeling shocked?

Well, I have got news for you. Money is even older than writing!

Yes, this is something that we know by looking at archaeological discoveries. Hieroglyphics or cuneiform are considered to be the oldest forms of writing. But when deciphered, most of these oldest writings turned out to be about money. They are the ledgers that our ancestors used to document their transactions. Hence, there is no doubt that money is even older than writing itself.

Wheels are often considered to be the first major technological invention in human civilization.

## Does money even predate the wheel?

Well, that is something that we do not know yet. Though it has been found that wheels were used as money in some ancient civilizations, whether it predates money is yet to be discovered.

Archaeologists around the world have concluded that money existed even in the Stone Age in the form of beads, feathers or shells.

Now that we have taken a look back at the history of money, what purpose do you think it actually serves? What is money actually? I think money has always been used as a form of communication. If you look at the very basic level, you will understand that money does not represent any value, rather it represents the notion of value. Money is the language through which we communicate value.

We actually use the money to value something. If you are buying a product, you are adding value to it by communicating with the seller with help of money. Money not only represents the notion of value, it also helps us to form social bonds with others. Thus, there is no doubt that money has a linguistic outlook as it is a form of communication too.

But above all, money is a technology first! Money is one of the first technologies that humankind created and it has evolved through the eras, yet money is one of the few technologies which are understudied.

Historian Niall Ferguson wrote in the book Ascent of Money:**"The ascent of money has been essential to the ascent of man."** And it is absolutely true!

Bitcoin is a big invention today and we all are mesmerized by everything that it offers. But it is actually a new form of money.

Let that sink in first!

## 2.1. HISTORY OF HUMAN MONETARY SYSTEM: THE EVOLUTION STORY

**Can you name a technology other than money that has changed its form several times throughout the history of human civilization?**

Well, I do not think anything has evolved as much as money. If you look at the very beginning, money was present in its non-abstract form. At that point in history, people used to exchange things in order to communicate value. Though money was not present in its physical form, the barter system that was used then was a monetary system too.

Let me explain it to you clearly.

## What do you do if you want to buy a dozen apples from the market?

You pay for a dozen apples.

However, things were a bit different when people used the barter system. They would basically exchange the products among themselves. So, if we had a barter system, you would probably have to exchange 1 dozen bananas to get 1 dozen apples. You get the picture.

### 2.1.1. The Beginning of Money – The Road to Coins

The first big evolution of money, as well as human civilization, started when people chose to exchange things which were not edible to communicate value. In the barter system, we saw that people generally used to exchange food items to communicate value among each other.

However, it changed completely when ancient people started exchanging stones, colorful objects or feathers to get what they needed. This was the exact moment in history when the abstract form of money that we know today came into being.

## Why was it a major transformation in the technology of money?

This was a major change because money was no longer about the consumption of the value. It became something that referred to a value; that is, an abstraction.

From the history books, we already know that the ancient kings of India, even during the Mughal Dynasty, used gold and silver coins as currency. However, the transformation from using beads or feathers to using precious metals for money was very long. It took thousands of years for human beings to start the next evolution of the technology of money after inventing its first abstract form.

## But why did it happen? Why did people opt for precious metals rather than stones or feathers?

The main reason behind this transformation was to have a stable monetary system. Now, let me explain it to you!

Let us suppose that you live in a place where crow's feathers are used as money. Is it hard to find a crow's feather? No, it is not! Anyone can find one. There is no control over the money and you can even cage some crows to have an endless supply of money.

When people have enough money (or crow feathers in this case) in their homes, why would they sell any product or service to get more money? And that is where the problem arises! If the money is uncontrolled and subjected to forgery, then it loses its value.

That was the main reason behind using precious metals as money. Gold, copper, and silver were hard to find and they were valued across the world for aesthetic purposes. So precious metals were melted and forged in the form of coins.

The first use of precious metals as coins was recorded in the ancient Mesopotamian civilization thousands of years ago. Since then all major civilizations including Greeks, Babylonians, Romans and ancient Indians have used precious metals to produce money.

## *2.1.2. A Bizarre Invention - The Paper Money*

It was a huge problem. If you think clearly then you will understand. Let me help you with it!

Suppose you sold me a few products and in return, I gave you a bag full of heavy coins. Would it be easy for you to carry them? Obviously, not!

The coins we use these days are much lighter than ancient currencies, but imagine carrying around a large sum only in coins. So, you can clearly understand the problem now!

Hence, someone formulated the brilliant idea of paper money. How did paper money come into existence?

Since gold was hard to carry, someone came up with the idea to trade paper rather than gold. Trusted institutions were created where people deposited their gold and in return, they were given pieces of paper with trusted seals. People started trading the paper in place of gold.

It was much easier for people to carry and handle the paper money. However, it brought a lot of skepticism along with it. Any invention or technological evolution draws skepticism. But I think the introduction of paper money made people most skeptical.

You will see that people who are somewhat technologically challenged freak out if they are told to do transactions online or in any way other than cash. So, can you imagine how people hundreds of years ago reacted when they were told to use paper money instead of gold? It was really unthinkable for them since they could not even figure out how a piece of paper could equal the value of a bag full of gold.

It took ages for people across the world to accept the notion of using paper as money and it helped the money technology to reach its next level.

## *2.1.3. The Invention of Plastic Money: The Game of Cards*

It was a few decades ago when we witnessed the rise of plastic cards as a new form of money. Nowadays, most people have a credit or debit card. But it also took several years for people to finally accept it.

The first credit card was created in the mid-1950s in the USA though it was nothing like the cards we use now. The first credit card was created in the form of the traveler's check.

But it gave rise to many controversies since everyday people refused to accept the traveler's check. If we take a close look at the evolution of money then this skepticism was nothing new. It took years for people to get acclimated to this new form of money.

As of today, it is accepted worldwide and it changed the monetary system completely.

## 2.1.4. Bitcoin: A new beginning?

Then, Bitcoin came along.

It was probably the biggest transformation in money technology since the rise of paper money. And people are still trying to get acclimated to it!

So, what is Bitcoin? Though we have talked about it in the previous chapter, here I will describe Bitcoin in terms of the historical context of money. Well, it is a form of money which is completely abstract.

Yes, Bitcoin took the technology of money to its highest point of abstraction.

So, let us formulate a definition of Bitcoin now!

Bitcoin can be simply described as the network-centric form of money.

And unfortunately, it does not make any sense as of now.

### Is it digital money then?

Of course, it is money in its digital form but Bitcoin is much more than just digital money. Furthermore, we have had digital money since long before Bitcoin came into being.

Thus, it is not right to categorize Bitcoin as digital money because it is much more than that.

Bitcoin is the future of money! It is the next big step towards the evolutionary process of money which has been continuing since the beginning of human civilization.

"Bitcoin was created to serve a highly political intent, a free and uncensored network where all can participate with equal access." – Amir Taaki, a Bitcoin developer

This is exactly what I am talking about!

**Bitcoin is a form of money that is seamless or boundary-less. It is simultaneous as well as translational! We have never seen a system of money like Bitcoin. Let me make this clear, it is not a payment system; it is a completely new monetary system.**

The money can be traded or transmitted instantaneously. Plus, there is one major thing that Bitcoin brought to this evolutionary process of money which we have never witnessed before.

Yes, it broke the boundaries of nations! Anyone can use this form of money which is indeed a great transformation.

Though it is far different from everything we have known before, Bitcoin will take money to its next stage.

# CHAPTER THREE

# SECURITY, STRENGTH, IDENTITY OR SURVEILLANCE? REASONS BEHIND THE RISE OF BITCOIN

We have discussed the need for a new value system and how Bitcoin fits into everything. Still, there is something that needs to be discussed.

## What makes Bitcoin so special? What is the reason behind the massive popularity of Bitcoin?

Here, I must make sure of one thing first. Whenever I use the term Bitcoin, I am not talking about the currency. I am talking about the completely decentralized network that powers Bitcoin.

A flat, decentralized network like Bitcoin is necessary to create a new value system. It is the next step that will replace the failing currency system of modern days.

Bitcoin is the future of the monetary system. So, it has to be special!

## 3.1. THE REDUNDANT BANKING SYSTEM: A GRAVE TRANSFORMATION OF A GREAT CREATION

Human beings have always restructured society by building or rebuilding essential institutions. But there is a problem with every institution that we build. Our institutions are hierarchical in nature and they essentially fail to evolve with time. The best examples of such institutions are the banks.

The process of banking was popularized from the early fourteenth century through the Renaissance and the industrial revolution. It helped people to become organized and communicate with each other on a much larger scale. Above all, it helped people to break free from the monopolies of the feudal lords and partake in the money system. But the system has become outdated now; it has become a mere imitation of the thing for which it was developed.

People often ask me to describe myself socio-politically; they want to know what my views are. I suppose this is the right time to answer that question. I consider myself a complete libertarian and a bit disruptarian.

### Why libertarian?

The thing is, I do not believe in the centralization of power. I believe in decentralized systems where the power lies in the hands of people themselves. Centralization of power is synonymous with corruption.

Throughout the course of human history, this is one of the things that we have observed in multiple instances. As a system becomes centralized, the power also gets centralized, and with this centralization of power, corruption happens.

## How can we solve this problem? How can we reboot the system and make it decentralized?

Well, the best way to achieve it is by simply disrupting things. Whenever power starts to become centralized, it is necessary to disrupt things to bring back order and transparency. And this is why I called myself a bit disruptarian.

The process of banking was developed to provide monetary power to the people. It was started as a liberator from feudal lords who had an almost monopoly over the financial system. Though the system once liberated billions of people from the traps of moneylenders and feudal lords, it is no longer a liberator.

With the passage of time, banks became centralized and they acquired absolute power over money which in turn corrupted the system. What we have today in the name of banks is not a liberating system, so it is time to disrupt it. And Bitcoin has the power to do this job efficiently.

**What do you think about that?**

## 3.2. NARROWING CIRCLE: REDUCED ACCESS TO THE BANKING SYSTEM

Over the last two decades, we have witnessed the transformation of the internet into a huge power of decentralization for communication. It has served as a great liberating force by disrupting the communication barriers among people.

However, if you look at the economy and banking system, we have not made much progress in terms of giving more access. As a matter of fact, we are regressing and economic inclusion is regressing too.

## Now, why is access to banking decreasing?

It is decreasing due to the architecture and isolated nature of modern-day finance. Barriers such as class structures, national borders, and attitudes toward money are further helping in this regression of access to banking.

Ironically, we live in a world where the global populace is becoming connected with the help of the internet. In fact, a global culture is emerging with the increasing popularity of the internet. Yet our monetary system is limited, hidebound and detached.

Since decentralized networks are an important part of our discussion, I want you to look at the existing banking system from the perspective of a network. If you judge the existing system from the network perspective, you will see there is a separate system for transacting small amounts, a separate system for large amounts, a separate system for B2B payments, a separate system for B2C transactions and so on.

There is a separate system for every transaction that you want to make. And these systems are separated by the nations, states, jurisdictions, and governments.

## Why is it so?

It simply means that we, the everyday people, are restricted from accessing the global financial system. The banks or the centralized bodies are restricting our access. Though global politics is to blame for this, it is simply ironical to see that the banks which were once considered to be the liberators have become the greatest limiters.

Thus, it is time to disrupt it all!

## 3.3. BITCOIN AND THE HOPE FOR BETTERMENT

The thing that makes Bitcoin so special is the fact that it provides flattened access to finance systems. The architecture of Bitcoin is doing for finance what the internet has done for communication. For example, if I have internet access, I will be able to get access to all the websites and facilities like everyone else having an internet connection.

Similarly, Bitcoin is providing the power of banking to everyone on a global scale. It will not distinguish between people on the basis of their nation, state or anything else; it will provide uniform access to everyone across the globe. It will create individually controlled banking by giving it the same stature as the largest bank in the world.

### What changes will Bitcoin make to the finance system?

Can you imagine yourself having the ability to execute transactions on a global scale, or create complex financial systems on your own without needing anyone else's permission? It seems impossible, doesn't it? Bitcoin helps you to achieve that. It's because Bitcoin runs on a decentralized network; you can start an application just by connecting to the network. This is something that you cannot do in any centralized system.

In a centralized system, if you are far away from it, then you will have less control over the process. However, if you move up the hierarchy of the system and get closer to it, then your access will be more restricted and limited. This is one of the major problems that Bitcoin eliminates. In a decentralized system like Bitcoin, every point in the system has equal access to the financial services.

It is not easy to start an application in a centralized network. You must have permission first. And remember this, permission is only granted if the application holds valid for a large populace and most importantly if it is profitable.

There is no need of that in Bitcoin. All it takes to start an application in this decentralized network are two people, two points, two systems and the binary codes that will start the application for you.

Two people can start transacting, creating their own protocols as well as their own systems in Bitcoin, and the application they start will be as valid as any other application in the Bitcoin network.

**How interesting does it sound?**

## 3.4. THE CALL FOR A NEUTRAL SYSTEM

Most people think that the true power of the internet lies in its ability to transmit information at a fast pace. However, that is not true at all! The true power of the internet lies in net neutrality.

**What is net neutrality?**

It is a special feature that the internet possesses. It does not discriminate on the basis of content, source or destination. You will get the same information as anyone else on this planet without any prejudice.

**But why are we talking about this while discussing Bitcoin?**

As a matter of fact, Bitcoin is a financial network that comes with net neutrality. While making a transaction in Bitcoin, the network does not pay any heed to the source of the transaction, the destination, the amount that is being transmitted or the application that is being used.

The only thing that the Bitcoin network cares about is whether you have provided sufficient funds to start using the resources that the network offers. If you have then your application is valuable as anyone else's.

## 3.5. DECENTRALISING MONEY

In the early 1970s, the world was first introduced to the concept of digital currency with the introduction of credit cards in the United States. Since then the world has started to adapt to it.

But it is not the same thing for Bitcoin. When people come to me and ask whether Bitcoin is a new digital currency, they miss the essential point. Even the dollar, euro or Indian rupee is a digital currency.

**Don't you transmit money using online wallets or internet banking?**

**Does not that make it a digital currency?**

Of course, it does! The fundamental difference of Bitcoin is that it runs an open-ended decentralized network while the digital currencies are a part of a centralized system.

As I have said before, Bitcoin is not a digital currency; it is a cryptocurrency. Though you have heard the term, let me explain what it actually means. It means Bitcoin is network-centric money.

As network-centric money, Bitcoin disposes of the requirements of the institutions, hierarchies and jurisdictions. All you need to do is to put your faith in the network.

The network itself is capable of solving the disagreements, boosting the security and performing all the necessary actions since no one is in control.

Above all, Bitcoin provides the utmost assurance of privacy for the transactions that you make. The blockchain network that Bitcoin uses is self-sufficient. It does not require permission from anyone to perform the actions. It is completely decentralized.

As I have said before, the blockchain network runs on mathematical problems and binary codes. No government, no authority and no financial institution have the power to breach the privacy of the transactions you make. You are the authority here and all power resides in you.

That's what makes Bitcoin special; that's the reason why it is becoming popular.

## 3.6. A CURRENCY FOR THE FUTURE

**What happens when the authorities are afraid of losing their power?**

They speak complete nonsense! The same thing happened back when the internet came into being. Since communication was slowly moving towards the decentralized network, the internet was shamed as a haven for terrorists, black marketers, and pedophiles. After twenty years, it is the greatest network of communication for the global populace.

The same thing is happening with Bitcoin. But you must always remember that it is the future of money. The biggest feature of the network-centric Bitcoin currency is that it is like a zombie; it is undead. Any currency, be it the euro, dollar or Indian rupee, it can be disbanded.

**Like what happened in India in 2016 during the demonetization!**

But that is not the case for Bitcoin. It automatically evolves with time and as we have mentioned before, it is not controlled by a centralized system. Thus, it will never become outdated. All it will have to do is survive and by the looks of it, this cryptocurrency is doing pretty well for itself.

**"We have an opportunity to reform the financial system, to turn it into the public utility that it's supposed to be—a level playing field that everyone can indiscriminately use in their bid to get ahead. Let that be the standard for the coming age of cryptocurrency,"** Paul Vigna wrote in his book The Age of Cryptocurrency: How Bitcoin and Digital Money Are Challenging the Global Economic Order. He was telling the truth!

Bitcoin is not just the internet money; it is the future.

Bitcoin is the future of money!

# CHAPTER FOUR

# PRINCIPLES OF BITCOIN DESIGN

I have talked about Bitcoin and its significance in the last chapters.

But let me remind you of something more important.

It is much more than just money. It is a technology. Bitcoin is a technology that is continuously evolving. It is making itself better at every instance. So, it is important that you understand the working and design principles of Bitcoin.

You already know that Bitcoin is different from any form of monetary system we ever had. It does not work on any centralized system rather the Bitcoin network is completely decentralized.

Instead of waiting for permission from any centralized authority, transactions in Bitcoin are carried out by mathematical interactions between two nodes in the system. Once a consensus is achieved between these two nodes, a transaction is made and it gets recorded in a digital ledger called a blockchain.

The terms and complicated explanations; it is getting pretty tough to understand, right?

Well, Bitcoin technology is a complicated one. It works on mathematical systems. So, if you want to understand the technicalities of Bitcoin then we may end up solving big equations.

Let's not go there!

It is better to analyze the design and working of Bitcoin through the eyes of a beginner in order to understand everything without frying the brain.

However, there is one thing that you must remember. Bitcoin is not an app or a software; it is a protocol. It is the future of the modern monetary system.

## 4.1. BITCOIN ARCHITECTURE: TIMESTAMP SERVER AND TRANSACTIONS

### How does the Bitcoin work?

Let us recall what we know so far!

Bitcoin transactions use cryptographic signatures to validate the transactions between two wallets. When a transaction is made, the system checks the cryptographic signature in the form of a mathematical proof coming from the owner of the wallet to validate it.

It all happens instantly and your transaction becomes successful without needing the permission of any central authority.

We know all this. However, we are only scratching the surface of the complicated process by telling the story of cryptographic signatures and mathematical proofs.

**It is not easy to run a system that is completely decentralized. Why is it so?**

It is because you are required to provide the proof of work at every instance; you will have to make sure that two nodes agree at the same moment about a transaction and it is necessary to develop a decentralized trust in order to get the system moving. This is much harder than you can imagine!

That explains why no one ever attempted to develop something like Bitcoin until the pseudonymous Satoshi Nakamoto published his solutions. It is true that we do not need to understand the complexities of the Bitcoin architecture.

But having a fair overall idea about the architecture of Bitcoin and its working is necessary to use this system in a better way.

### 4.1.1. Understanding Transactions in Bitcoin

First of all, answer one simple question.

**What is a transaction in Bitcoin? How can you answer it in the simplest terms?**

Well, a transaction is the transfer of currency from one wallet to another existing in the Bitcoin network. This is actually what the transaction in Bitcoin is all about.

However, it is not the easiest thing to do without having any centralized trust.

At the same time, it is not impossible to do and Bitcoin is the biggest proof of that.

In Bitcoin, every coin is simply defined as a chain of electronic signatures. And every transaction is made by combining these signatures.

Let us take an example to understand Bitcoin in a better way.

Suppose I have a Bitcoin wallet. Now, my sister has asked me to transfer some amount into her Bitcoin wallet. Well, how will the transaction happen? She lives in New York City and I cannot travel overseas at this time to give her the money.

Here, one thing you must remember. When you are opening a wallet in Bitcoin, you are provided with one public and one private key.

So, when I am transferring the money, the Bitcoin network will check my private key against the public key of my sister's wallet to approve the transfer. Once the system verifies and approves the transaction, the money will be transferred immediately.

## But why does Bitcoin need the digital key? Why can't the money be simply transferred by probing the public key of the recipient?

It is because there is no centralized system. In any centralized system, the value is added to the transfer by the authority. How will you do that in a completely decentralized network of Bitcoins? Well, it is done by verifying the private keys.

As I said before, the private key is the output or the hash of the previous transaction. The coins are designed in such a way that they draw value from the hash of the previous transaction. (See section below for an explanation if "hash" is a new term for you.)

Therefore, by only signing the hash of the previous transaction digitally, you will be able to add value to the amount that you are attempting to transfer.

In simple words, if you do not have a private key then you will never be allowed to do transactions. This way the Bitcoin protocol also offers utmost security to users.

But this decentralized network also creates a problem for us.

### 4.1.2. Function of Timestamp Server

There is still a major problem that is left unanswered. How will you ensure that you are not double spending? How will you make sure that you are not doing the same transaction twice?

This is something really complicated to ensure since there is no centralized system. In other words, it seems almost impossible to do in the decentralized Bitcoin network.

That leads us to our next pillar of Bitcoin's design.

The timestamp server!

The timestamp server was the solution that Satoshi Nakamoto proposed in his paper regarding the problem that I mentioned just above. The timestamp server was shown as the key to prevent the problems of double spending.

**Now, the question is how? How did they do it? How did the developers of Bitcoin use the timestamp server to solve the problem of double spending?**

If we just analyze the architecture of the internet then we will be better able to understand the timestamp server. It is not impossible to think that a data might have existed on the database of the internet at some point in time. That data can be reused again for your work to be completed.

The working of the timestamp server is somewhat similar. The server checks whether a data exists in the network about a previous transaction. If there is any existing data then the timestamp server checks it and uses it to prevent the problem of double spending.

I have already told you about the blockchain ledger that the Bitcoin protocol uses to have a record of all the transactions that you do. And it obviously plays a big role in providing the proof of work to prevent the problem of double spending.

In the blockchain ledger, each timestamp includes its previous timestamp in a hash (a simple block in a mapping function). Thus, it forms a chain with each timestamp reinforcing the ones that came before it.

As a matter of fact, you can actually afford to forget the working of the timestamp server. You can just remember that the blockchain ledger provides the mathematical proof to the system; as a result, it prevents the problem of double spending.

### *4.1.3. Comprehending The Bitcoin Network*

To understand the principle of Bitcoin design, it is better to understand the Bitcoin network first.

**Have you seen the human nervous system?**

It looks like a complex network of nerves starting from the brain with certain neural nodes that oversee the work of the nervous system. Well, the Bitcoin network is something similar to the nervous system with the exception of having a centralized authority like the brain.

The point of making this comparison is to tell you that the Bitcoin network consists of nodes. The nodes act as the most vital points in this decentralized network as they do all the hard work to keep this protocol running without any hindrance.

## So, how does the Bitcoin network work?

The network simply works by broadcasting the essential information from a new transaction to all the nodes. Is it all? Are there no other hidden processes or anything? Well, of course, there are, but in an overview, this is how the Bitcoin network works.

Let me give you the simplest explanation.

As soon as the nodes receive the broadcast of new transactions, they collect all necessary data from the new transactions in the form of blocks. Then each node starts to dig the blockchain ledger for finding the proof of work. When the proof of work is found, the node that finds it broadcasts the block to all other nodes.

The nodes only accept the block after verifying the proof of work. What do they verify? They check whether the transaction has already happened or if it is valid. Only upon proper verification, the nodes accept the block. As soon as the block is accepted by the nodes, it gets added to the blockchain and a hash of the block (a new private key) is generated for facilitating the next transaction.

This is all there is to the working of the Bitcoin network. Thus, the cryptographic keys, timestamp server and proof of work, these are the three main things that form a block which provides the mathematical proofs required to carry out a transaction and keep the Bitcoin network running without the need for any centralized authority.

## 4.2. BLOCKCHAIN TECHNOLOGY: EVERYTHING YOU NEED TO KNOW

**"The blockchain is an incorruptible digital ledger of economic transactions that can be programmed to record not just financial transactions but virtually everything of value."** Don and Alex Tapscott wrote this line in their 2016 book, Blockchain Revolution.

And this is the exact truth that comes to my mind when I hear about blockchain technology. The blockchain technology is the key to the rise of Bitcoin. It is actually the thing that makes Bitcoin so special and interesting in the first place.

As TedX speaker and technology futurist Ian Khan says: "As revolutionary as it sounds, Blockchain truly is a mechanism to bring everyone to the highest degree of accountability. No more missed transactions, human or machine errors, or even an exchange that was not done with the consent of the parties involved.

Above anything else, the most critical area where Blockchain helps is to guarantee the validity of a transaction by recording it not only on the main register but a connected distributed system of registers, all of which are connected through a secure validation mechanism."

The blockchain is basically nothing but a public ledger. It stores all the data regarding the transactions made from one wallet to another. It is similar to the database that the internet has which stores all the information.

Similarly to the internet, the Bitcoin system uses the blockchain ledger to retrieve any information necessary.

As I explained before, the Bitcoin network uses the cryptographic keys, timestamps, and proof of work to efficiently perform the transactions without the need for any centralized authority. And the blockchain is the key to this mechanism.

Once a new transaction is facilitated, the data from the new transaction is broadcast to all the nodes in the network as I have explained before. But the things that happen after that, from retrieving the proof of work to validating the transaction, everything is done with the help of a blockchain ledger.

It provides all necessary information to the nodes. And once the transaction is complete, a new block gets added to the chain with the record of the latest transaction.

The blockchain ledger not only brings efficiency to the Bitcoin network. It also makes it robust and secured. Why am I saying this? Well, it is because the blockchain network is protected by cryptographic encryption which not even the finest hackers can break. Above all, it disposes of the need of any third party. Thus, it keeps your information private and secured.

I have always said that Bitcoin is not a payment system or currency, it is a technology.

Now, you know why!

# CHAPTER FIVE

# AN INTRODUCTION TO THE WALLETS AND THE COINS: GETTING STARTED WITH BITCOIN

## What have you learned so far about Bitcoin?

I have discussed the significance of Bitcoin in the world today and how it is revolutionizing the modern value system. I also showed you how the Bitcoin transaction works in the last chapter.

## What next?

Well, now we are starting the most exciting part of the book. Yes, I am going to show you the path to get started with Bitcoin.

The process is not at all complicated. All you will have to do is to get a few coins and store them in a wallet. Yes, that's all you need to do.

As I have said several times before, Bitcoin offers a great opportunity for investors too. It is not just an ordinary payment system or a digital currency. Though it is true that volatility exists in Bitcoin too, the risk of losing money is much less than in any other investment option currently available in the market.

So, if you are having second thoughts about getting started with Bitcoin, it is the right time to make up your mind.

## 5.1. WHAT ARE BITCOIN WALLETS?

Let me ask you a question.

**What is the very first thing you need to do to start with Bitcoin?**

**Register to Bitcoin? Create an online Bitcoin account?**

**Aren't these the things that you usually do to get started with any online application?**

Well, Bitcoin is not a web-based application or a website. As I have said before, it is a protocol that uses mathematical formulas to have its work done.

Now the question is what do you need to do first? The answer is simple; you need to create a Bitcoin wallet for yourself.

## "Wait! A Bitcoin wallet? Isn't this similar to the online wallets we use?"

This is obviously the very first thing that comes to your mind. Honestly, they are not the same.

A Bitcoin wallet is a very first step that you need to take to access the Bitcoin network. If you do not own a wallet then you will never be able to use the Bitcoin protocol to deposit or transact money.

It is not too different from the banking system that we have. You need to have a bank account to use banking facilities.

Similarly, you will have to own a Bitcoin wallet to enjoy the facilities that Bitcoin offers.

As a matter of fact, the wallets do not store Bitcoins; rather the wallets come with the public as well as private keys and codes which are stored in the wallets. These private keys and codes help you to transact in the Bitcoin network. They need to be stored securely since they give you access to the Bitcoins you store.

But the Bitcoin wallets are different types and each comes with its own set of advantages as well as disadvantages. You can store your Bitcoin in the cold storage that is on the hardware as well as paper wallets. And there are also hot wallets like software and online wallets too. Hence, you will have to understand what you need first.

## So, which type of wallet is perfect for you?

I will explain them all, but then leave it for you to figure out!

### *5.1.1. Hardware wallets*

As I said earlier, you will have to understand the types of wallets available very well. The first type of wallet that you need to know about is the hardware wallet.

## What is a hardware wallet?

A hardware wallet is basically nothing but a physical electronic device. It looks very similar to the flash drives that you own to store important files or backup of your computer data. However, these hardware wallets are designed with the sole purpose of storing the Bitcoins.

The excellent thing about these wallets is that they need to be connected to your mobile, tablet or PC before you carry out any transaction in Bitcoins.

If you are really serious about the security of your Bitcoins, then the hardware wallets are indeed a great choice. They are reliable as well as convenient. But the best thing about the hardware wallets is that they keep the private keys in a completely separate offline device away from the vulnerable devices that are connected to the internet.

Since your private key gives you access to your Bitcoins, hackers can access your online wallets and steal your private key. Thus, as far as security is concerned, there is nothing that comes close to the hardware wallet.

If you generate as well as store Bitcoins in a hardware wallet then the cyber-criminals will have no way to access them. Plus, these wallets also come with a security PIN. Hence, even if your hardware wallet gets stolen, hackers will never be able to decrypt the security encryption on it to access your Bitcoins.

The hardware wallets are also very easy to use and the chances of error are very low even for technically challenged users. Nevertheless, there is still one thing that drives many users away from the hardware wallets. The hardware wallets are not free; you will have to buy them for a fixed price.

If you are willing to spend some money to ensure maximum security then there is nothing better than the hardware wallets.

### *5.1.2. Paper wallets*

As the name suggests, the paper wallets are nothing more than a piece of paper. Having a paper wallet is perhaps the cheapest option available.

The paper wallets are nothing but a document containing the public and the private keys which form a wallet. The best thing about paper wallets is that they come with QR codes which you can easily scan to obtain the keys in order to facilitate a transaction in Bitcoin.

With the paper wallets, you will never have to worry about cyber attacks or hardware device failure. If you keep the paper safely without any degradation then it is obviously one of the best wallet options available.

But how will you generate a paper wallet? You cannot buy it from a store, that's for sure. So, what will you have to do? Any guesses?

It is not something highly complicated to do. Just visit a site where you can generate a secured Bitcoin address (bitaddress.org and blockchain.info are some examples). Just follow the instructions that appear on the screen of your device.

When you are done creating your paper wallet, just download it in the form of a PDF file. Take a printout of your PDF document on a good quality paper and you are done creating your paper wallet.

However, there are few things that you need to keep in mind once you create your paper wallet. A piece of paper is one of the most fragile things on the face of the earth and the ink on the paper can degrade over time. So, you will have to keep the paper very carefully. Moreover, you must protect the paper from being folded, and from water and other things that can destroy it.

**Why am I stressing so much on keeping the paper with utmost safety?** Well, if you lose the paper or if it gets destroyed somehow, you will never be able to access the bitcoins that are stored at that particular address.

All things considered, the paper wallets are very fragile and that is a disadvantage. But you can laminate the paper to keep it protected.

Paper wallets are easy to use and you will have no trouble creating one for yourself.

### 5.1.3. Web-based wallets

Yes, there are web-based Bitcoin wallets too. But these are nothing similar to anything you have used.

The online wallets store the private key in a completely secured server. There are several online wallet services available these days and they are highly secured. So, you will not have to worry about the security of your access keys.

## What is the greatest advantage that the online wallets offer?

The best thing about the online wallet is that you will be able to access it anywhere at any time. If you are connected to the internet then you will always have access to your wallet. And these wallets are not at all device specific. Regardless of the device that you are using, you will always have access to your online wallet.

However, the online wallets have their own set of disadvantages too. Most of these wallets are operated by an organization and they often give themselves full control over your private key. Thus, these companies start behaving like the banks.

Of course, it is really scary and it becomes much scarier when you start using a large number of Bitcoins. The Bitcoin protocol was originally developed to make the monetary system free from the chains of centralized power, so these kinds of acts are completely unforgivable.

As a result, you will have to make sure that the online wallet service that you are using does not have control over your private key.

### 5.1.4. Software wallet

This is the last type of hot wallets!

The software wallets can further be divided into desktop and mobile wallets. You can choose the wallet option that suits all your requirements.

First, let's have a look at the desktop wallets. As the name suggests, the desktop wallets are meant to be run on a desktop and they are very easy to use actually. All you have to do is to download and install a Bitcoin client on your computer.

A desktop wallet allows you to create a Bitcoin address apart from transacting in Bitcoins.

The mobile wallets, though, are actually more convenient in modern times. With the mobile wallets, you will always have access to your Bitcoin wallet as long as you have your mobile with you. The mobile wallets are available in the form of apps for your smartphone.

The mobile wallets are designed in such a way that they do not download the entire blockchain as they can create memory problems.

The software wallets are pretty convenient to use but they are mostly device specific which can create problems later on.

**Can you see why?**

## 5.2. HOW TO BUY BITCOINS?

Well, you now know how to get yourself a Bitcoin wallet. But that's only the first step!

The second step to get started with Bitcoin is much more complicated.

## How to buy Bitcoins?

There are no shops where you can just buy them. Then, what will you do? How will you add Bitcoins to your wallet?

You will have to buy them from exchanges or online wallets. As a matter of fact, there are several exchanges as well as wallets available where you will be able to buy Bitcoins.

However, it is always better to do it in a bureaucratic way; that is, by providing your personal details. In India, for example, it is important to fulfill the KYC requirements and I make sure to do so since it is better than being anonymous. It secures you from money laundering and protects your interests completely.

You can easily buy Bitcoins from these exchanges or wallets by using your debit cards issued by Visa or MasterCard. You can also use net banking facilities to purchase Bitcoins directly from your bank account. Make sure that your card uses a 3D payment security system before making the purchase.

Pocketbits.co.in is one of the leading Bitcoin exchange in India. You can easily register here with your PAN details. Another thing, you will be able to buy Bitcoins from this exchange by transferring the money through NEFT or RTGS apart from card transactions.

Well, now you know how to get started with Bitcoin. Now, it is your decision whether you want to move forward with Bitcoin.

**"If you don't believe it or don't get it, I don't have the time to try to convince you, sorry."** – Satoshi Nakamoto, the creator of Bitcoin

Whether you believe in Bitcoin is completely up to you. No one will ever force you to get started with Bitcoin. If you join the beautiful network of Bitcoin, you will surely be able to accomplish wonders.

# CHAPTER SIX

# INVESTING IN BITCOIN: THE GOOD, THE BAD AND EVERYTHING YOU SHOULD KNOW

## It is a beautiful day for making good investments! Don't you agree?

Well, it must be done very carefully with a proper strategy.

I have already told you what Bitcoin is; its importance and why it is a good investment option. We have also discussed creating a wallet and buying Bitcoins.

Therefore, it only leads us in one direction.

## How to make investments in Bitcoin?

This is a question that has troubled many people. The Bitcoin market is highly volatile. As a result, understanding the right time to invest in this cryptocurrency as well as finding the right way to do so is really a troublesome job.

Nevertheless, it is still the smartest investment that you can make. The Bitcoin protocol was programmed to grow without being bound to any limit. It was designed to prevent people from being cheated. Though the prices of Bitcoin fluctuate at times, it is still the best investment option for you.

Since there is no centralized authority to govern it, the Bitcoin is programmed to help you grow and earn the profit.

I wonder why!

## 6.1. THE ADVANTAGES AND DISADVANTAGES OF BITCOIN INVESTMENT

Investing money is all about understanding your risk appetite. Yes, you need to have a proper idea of the amount of money that you can afford to lose.

Once you have a clear idea of that, making smart investments becomes very easy. You will have to do the same while investing in Bitcoin.

Every platform has its fair share of advantages as well as disadvantages and we all know these things very well. Bitcoin is not an exception. Investing in Bitcoin has its own disadvantages too.

But the question is how significant are these disadvantages? Is it worth taking the risk to invest in Bitcoin?

I will outline the pros and cons, but then I'll leave this for you to answer.

### *6.1.1. The Advantages of Investing in Bitcoin:*

The biggest advantage of Bitcoin lies in its decentralized structure. In other words, the decentralized structure of Bitcoin is its biggest asset.

As I have said earlier, in any centralized system the power lies completely in the hands of the centralized authority which leads to corruption and laundering of money. That was the main motive behind the creation of this brilliant technology.

Since there is no central authority to guide its action, the power lies within the system itself and all the works in this system are done by solving complex mathematical problems.

## Now, the question is, how does that help in making investments?

Since Bitcoin is not governed by any financial institution or bank, the worth of BTC does not depend on the ruling of a centralized authority. Of course, the currency can and does fluctuate; these are the only factors that affect the worth of Bitcoins.

Another thing that makes Bitcoin so valuable and special is its scarcity. Bitcoin is very similar to gold in this aspect.

## What makes gold so valuable?

The gold reserves in the world are fixed. We cannot produce an unlimited quantity of gold. The artificial methods of producing gold are not actually feasible and this scarcity is what makes gold so precious as a metal.

**The same thing goes for Bitcoin! Bitcoin is not a resource which can be generated whenever the demand becomes high. The Bitcoin network creates the units at a very steady rate and it will continue to do so until it reaches its limit at 21 million units.**

You heard it right! The system will produce 21 million units at most and that is the limit. There will never be another BTC produced by the system. Thus, the resources are scarce. And once the system hits its finish line, the supply of Bitcoin will not be in sync with the demand.

## What happens when the supply becomes limited and the demand becomes sky high?

I believe you know the answer all too well.

Since this scarcity exists, the price or value of Bitcoin will always remain valuable. In fact, it will continue to increase as the resources become scarcer.

So, you may earn huge amounts for even the small investments that you make today.

**Do you see now how promising it is to invest in BTC?**

## *6.1.2. Disadvantages of investing in Bitcoin:*

As I said before, everything has a disadvantage too and Bitcoin is no exception.However, I must tell you that the so-called cons of Bitcoin are nothing serious or new. You are familiar with these disadvantages.

As several cryptocurrency enthusiasts point out, Bitcoin is highly volatile and it is not backed up by any legal protection. Many experts believe that the fluctuations in the value of Bitcoin are much more than any currency that is controlled by a government.

Furthermore, there are several uncertainties regarding the future of Bitcoin. Will there be any government intervention to control this cryptocurrency? What will happen to Bitcoin once it hits the 21 million cap? And the list goes on!

But seriously, is there really anything to be concerned about? I will let you decide that.

However, the real problem that still exists with Bitcoin is the scalability issue. If this scalability issue is solved then the transactions in Bitcoin will be much smoother and hassle-free for the system.

## 6.1.3. Should you invest in Bitcoin?

**So, after all this, is it worth investing in Bitcoin?**

Let me hear what you think!

You have seen the pros; so you can understand that the value of Bitcoin will only increase with the time. I can guarantee you that.

**But what about the concerns that some people have about Bitcoin?**

**Don't you think those are absurd?**

The main point behind the creation of Bitcoin was to create a value system which is not governed by any central authority. This is what makes Bitcoin what it is today.

Moreover, volatility exists in every liquidity market and Bitcoin is no exception. Even though it is volatile, the price of BTC will only increase as I mentioned before. As a result, these concerns are really of no value.

The real problem is that most people do not understand what Bitcoin is, yet they do not stop making comments. It is very similar to what happened when the internet was first introduced to the world.

People resent changes and it can be seen throughout the course of human history. Still, we cannot stop ourselves from evolving and Bitcoin is the next big step in our evolution. It is the flag bearer of the evolution of our value system.

**So, I ask you again; is it worth investing in Bitcoin?**

I think you will be able to answer this question in a better way. No wonder why!

## 6.2. THE STRATEGY OF MAKING BITCOIN INVESTMENT:

Now that you have understood that Bitcoin is the best way to invest your money, let me ask you one question.

### How do you plan to invest in Bitcoin?

Yes, you must have a good plan of investment like any other smart investor. So, what is your "big badass strategy"?

I know; you still do not have one. Well, let's formulate one for you!

The investment that you make in Bitcoin depends completely upon the financial asset that you have. Of course, calculating the investment that you should make depends completely on the financial asset that you have and your risk appetite.

The general notion is that you can invest 1-10% of your total financial asset in Bitcoin. However, if you have a high-risk appetite then you can invest 30% or even 50-70% of your financial asset in Bitcoin.

### But what is a financial asset?

I think this is something we must discuss before proceeding further. A financial asset is not liquid cash that you have in your hand. Neither am I talking about physical assets like property and cars nor anything valuable you may have at your home. By financial asset, I simply mean the money that you have saved throughout your life in the form of bank balance, investments in share markets, mutual funds or bonds.

### How will you understand the right amount of money that you need to invest in Bitcoin?

If your financial asset is within the range of $10,000 to $100,000 then it is always wise to invest 1-10% of your financial asset in Bitcoin as per your risk appetite. I am summing your financial assets in the dollar since it is a standard currency. Just as I said, if your assets fall within this range then investing 1-10% of your asset in Bitcoin is the wisest move that you can make.

However, if your financial asset is more than $100,000, you can take a little more risk and go up to 40 or 50%. Above all, everything depends on your risk appetite. The amount of risk that you are willing to take will always be the scale for measuring the money that you invest.

But you always need to be smart and that matters even more than the financial asset you have. This is one virtue that every investor must have. How will you be a smart Bitcoin investor? Just remember the 5% rule.

## 5% rule?

Yes, the 5% rule will help you to make smart investments even if you do not have a huge financial asset.

So, what does this 5% rule tell you? If you have a steady flow of income, then invest 5% of your financial asset in Bitcoin. Once you get a good return then add 5% more to the amount that you have invested. In this way, increase the amount that you invest by 5% without having to take a huge risk. Above all, you can always curtail the amount you invest at any time without any hassle.

**Now that is a pretty smart move, isn't it?**

### *6.2.1. What should you know to invest money?*

We have formulated the smartest strategy to invest in Bitcoin. However, it still does not answer one little question. How will you invest the money? What will you have to do to invest in Bitcoin?

Actually, investing money in Bitcoin is pretty simple and there is no hidden trick to it.

All you will have to do is to buy BTC from exchanges or wallets. Once you have bought the BTC with your money, just keep it stored in your wallet.

## Now, how long will you store the money in the wallet?

Store it as long as you get a good price for the Bitcoins you have in your wallet. That means just sell the BTC when the market is high to gain great profits.

That's all there is to the Bitcoin investment. Of course, you can also invest in the Bitcoin mining but that is a topic for another time.

## 6.3. IMPORTANT SUGGESTIONS FOR MAKING BITCOIN INVESTMENT

You now know everything that you need to invest in Bitcoin. So, I think it is important to give you some expert tips that you can leverage while making investments.

- **Do your homework first about the current market condition and check the projected future of the Bitcoin rate before making the investment. This way you will be able to fully utilize the Bitcoin network.**

- **Understand your risk appetite properly.**

- **Just use the exchanges for buying or selling Bitcoins. But do not keep your coins there since they can be targeted by cybercriminals. Keep your coins safe in your wallet and sell them when the market is high to get a good return.**

"Investing money is the process of committing resources in a strategic way to accomplish a specific objective." Alan

Gotthardt wrote this in his book The Eternity Portfolio and this is something that every investor must understand.

Bitcoin is the future of investments too. So, be smart and understand your risks first then you will be able to accomplish wonders.

There is no doubt in that!

# CHAPTER SEVEN

# THE CURRENT PAIN OF MONEY TRANSFER AND BANK A/Cs

## What do you think of the banking system today?

It is really bad, isn't it? Waiting in lines to deposit money, repeated failure of server links, high transfer rates for transferring money to an account in a different bank, high exchange rates to transfer money abroad and the list of problems we face continues.

Yes, we all have faced these problems for a long time. And it needs to change!

The name of that change is Bitcoin. As I have stated several times before, Bitcoin is the future of banking and payment systems. It is the future of money and the next step in human evolution.

The banking industry today limits the access of people to the economy. It does not allow everyday people to participate in the world economy and keeps the power to itself. However, this was never meant to happen. This authoritarian behavior of the financial institutions of the modern day inspired the creation of Bitcoin.

Bitcoin is not just a payment system or digital currency; it is an invention, or rather a technology which is specifically designed to shatter the chains and liberate the people. I wonder why!

## 7.1. WHY THE MODERN DAY BANKING SYSTEM HAS BECOME PAINFUL?

The creation of banks was a landmark in the history of humankind. It was the first step that our ancestors took to restructure the society.

Before the origin of banks during the Renaissance period, the monetary system was controlled by the feudal lords. The everyday people used to take money from the feudal lords and the interest rates were very high.

The feudal system was faulty in different ways. Above all, it led to the exploitation of the normal populace. It is often said that money is power. So, the feudal lords became very powerful which brought the dark ages in medieval Europe.

With the Renaissance and the industrial revolution, social reformers took the first steps to liberate the common people from the manacles of the feudal system. Of course, the banks were created to liberate people and to allow them to participate freely in the economy. The banks were liberators!

There was another reason for the creation of the banks. As I have said in a previous chapter, carrying gold or silver coins around was actually very painful. So, banks were created as safe havens where people could safely store their money and receive certificates or bank notes in return which could be used for paying for goods and services. As you may have already understood by now, it was the forerunner of modern payment systems.

However, it did not take much time for the banks to become limiters rather than liberators. Actually, if we analyze correctly then we can understand that the main problem lies in the structure of the banking system. The banking system that we have today is hierarchical in design and that's what creates the problem in the first place.

In every hierarchical system, there is a central authority which has all the power. Our banks are no different! They have a total control over the currency which provides them with immense power. Thus, it creates problems for the common populace.

Everyday people today are not allowed to participate in the world economy. It is fair to say that their access is very limited. Suppose you want to transfer some money to your brother who lives in New York City. To make a wire transfer to New York, you will have to follow the hazardous procedures of the bank and the exchange rates as well as the taxes. This will normally discourage anyone from going through the process ever again.

You are wasting your time as well as money on taxes and other charges. What does it bring to you? It brings nothing but disappointment!

Furthermore, the experience of day-to-day banking is bitter too. For example, what do you need to do open an account in a government bank in India? You will have to apply for your bank account by filling out forms and submitting a great load of your personal documents. Then the bank will verify your documents, your address and after a long procedure of verification, your application will be approved.

It is not finished there; not yet! Once your application is approved, you will have to wait for few days before your account gets active. Furthermore, you generally will have to maintain a minimum balance to keep your bank account active and to avoid penalties. Plus, the payment transfer system is frustrating irrespective of how digitized it has become.

If you need to transfer money from your account to a different account in a different bank, you will have to pay high charges. There are other problems with the poor infrastructure of the banks.

Often, we face huge problems due to server failures in the bank and this just makes everything worse. Huge lines at ATMs is another problem that every one of us faces in our daily lives.

Actually, there is no end to the complaints we have against the banking system that we have today. This centralized system has run its course. It has become obsolete and it needs to be disrupted. The financial institutions have grown in power and they have diverted from the purpose for which they were originally created.

Yes, they have become limiters! I have always said that I consider myself as a disruptor and a liberator. This is the right time for us to take steps forward; we call for the change. It is time we disrupt this failing and corrupt banking system to embrace the light.

It is time for us to embrace Bitcoin. Bitcoin was created to become a beacon of hope to the people who are suffering from the pain of this corrupt banking and payment transfer system. So, it is your cue to make the right choice!

## 7.2. IS BITCOIN THE ANSWER TO TODAY'S BANKING PROBLEMS?

You have become quite familiar with the term Bitcoin by now.

## What do you think of this amazing technological invention?

It is not a place to just invest your money to get a great return; neither is it just a digital currency that you can use for your own purpose. Honestly, Bitcoin is all of these and much more! It is the wind of change that is about to set us free from the painful manacles of the corrupted banking system. It is a single currency for people all over the world.

Bitcoin is the future; it is the beginning of a new age.

## Now, why do you need to switch to Bitcoin? What makes it so much better than the existing banking system?

Let us start from the very beginning!

Bitcoin was created to free the monetary system from a centralized authority. Of course, Bitcoin does not have a centralized authority. It is a protocol that uses some variables and mathematical functions to work. Bitcoin does not require any authority to govern its work and the power lies in the system itself.

When you transfer BTC from your wallet to someone else's wallet, the system checks for the cryptographic signatures. If the signatures match and the system approves the transaction then the balance will be transferred without any hassle. This is the main thing that makes Bitcoin so special!

Bitcoin is not hierarchical in design, rather it has a liberal design. Thus, it guarantees that it will provide you the freedom to transact money across the world without being limited by authoritarian rules.

This brings us to the next most important thing about Bitcoin. Bitcoin is a currency too!

## But how does it differ from the dollar, pound, Euro, Indian rupee and others?

Bitcoin is a universal currency. This is where it differs from everything else. Being universal means it is the same for people all over the world. You can transact in Bitcoin from anywhere in the world without caring about the borders or exchange rates.

If you need to transfer money to a loved one living abroad, Bitcoin will help you to do that without any hassle. There are no extra charges and there is no need to worry about the transfer rates; you will be able to complete the transaction from your house.

Bitcoin encourages people to participate in the world economy rather limiting their access to it. This is the second reason why Bitcoin wins over the system of banking and payments that we have today.

As far as the security of your money is concerned, Bitcoin has outsmarted the banks and other payments systems in this aspect too. Bitcoin uses a digital public ledger called blockchain to keep a record of the transactions that are happening in Bitcoin. It is available to the public, so you can see it but there is no way to tamper with it.

**The encryption of the blockchain network is virtually impossible to crack. Thus, there is no government, cybercriminal or any third party who can tamper with your Bitcoins. It provides you with the most security that you could ask for, and I can totally vouch for it.**

Many people often ask me whether it is possible to use Bitcoin in their daily lives as they use their credit or debit cards. There are people who still believe that this is one thing that makes the existing banking system better than Bitcoin.

They are wrong!

You can easily use Bitcoin to shop online. Furthermore, many local stores, malls and department stores have started to accept Bitcoin. So, you can use this cryptocurrency to buy anything you want in place of your credit or debit cards. Do you know what the good thing about it is? Well, you will not have to pay any charges which the cards issued by the banks are subjected to. Hence, you will actually be saving money by using BTC in place of the normal currency.

There is no end to the advantages that Bitcoin offers. It is a revolution that will change our value system and it has already begun.

**Do you still wonder why Bitcoin is better than the banks?**

## 7.3. LEGAL OR ILLEGAL: THE VERDICT ON BITCOIN

I have heard many people or agencies saying Bitcoin is illegal and that it will become the source of black money and terrorism.

Well, there is no need to worry about that! If you think closely then you will understand that these are the same things those people said when the internet was created.

The internet brought the same kind of change to the communication system. It made gathering information or connecting with people across the world easy. It freed communication from the chains of the authorities.

Bitcoin is doing the same thing with the value system. Bitcoin is freeing it from the chains.

As a result, we are witnessing these uproars. Actually, the banks or financial institutions that hold immense power are scared. Yes, they are scared of losing their power! Bitcoin is bringing the wind of change along with it and it will abolish the centralized authorities for once and all.

This has made them scared which in return is provoking them to create these rumors against Bitcoin. However, they are baseless completely. When you create a wallet or buy BTC, you will have to submit a Know Your Customer or KYC form with your identification proofs. Thus, there is nothing illegal about it. As I said, these are baseless rumors created to confuse people.

Do not let yourself be intimidated by that and be a part of this great change! Disrupt the corrupted banking system and embrace Bitcoin.

"**At its core, bitcoin is a smart currency designed by very forward-thinking engineers. It eliminates the need for banks, gets rid of credit card fees, currency exchange fees, money transfer fees, and reduces the need for lawyers in transitions... all good things.**" This is something *Peter Diamandis*, an American businessman, said about Bitcoin a few years back.

Well, I think we all would agree with what he said.

Wouldn't you?

**CHAPTER EIGHT**

# BITCOIN: IS IT A THREAT OR A GIFT?

We have covered so many important topics so far. We have discussed blockchain technology, Bitcoin's working process, how to invest in Bitcoin and above all, the relevance of this technology in modern society.

I believe this is the perfect opportunity to answer the question that has been at the center of an ongoing debate for a long time.

**What is Bitcoin in reality? Is it a threat to society? Or is it a gift that has been entrusted to us?**

If you are active on the internet and social media, you may have noticed by now that a very enthralling debate has been going on among the experts about understanding the full capabilities of Bitcoin. While most people have welcomed it as a revolutionary technology that our failing value system needs, there are also those who have expressed their fears that Bitcoin may become a reason for a great socio-economic disaster in the near future.

Though this debate will continue, I will unravel what the actual reality of Bitcoin is. With the help of examples and taking a broader perspective, we will understand whether Bitcoin is really a gift or a threat to modern society.

## 8.1. THE SKEPTICISM AROUND BITCOIN: A HISTORICAL APPROACH

The difference in perspectives and the debate about how the abilities of Bitcoin will turn out is nothing new to us. We have faced similar situations before.

If you take a look back at our history, you will find that such debates have originated whenever the world has come across a new invention. Be it Galileo inventing the telescope or the evolution of paper money, such skeptics have always been there.

But I do not need to take you centuries back, let us just go to the early '90s and we will have the best example to relate to this ongoing debate about Bitcoin.

It was around 1992 when the first web browser was introduced to the world. Though the internet was a few years old by that time, the concept of the web was just beginning. The world was introduced to the web with the help of the first-ever web browser, NCSA Mosaic. Today, we have several web browsers at our disposal. However, it was very different back then and installing the NCSA Mosaic web browser was nothing less than a hassle.

Researchers around the world worked for hours in their labs to download, compile and install the browser on their computers. As they launched the browser after completing the hefty installation process, the researchers were presented with an astonishing experience. Well, it usually took hours to just visit a website back then but experiencing the web for the first time was really enlightening for many.

However, the controversies were waiting just around the corner. The invention that changed the internet was labeled as a threat by many technological enthusiasts. They even went further to call it the "tool for destruction of the world." Many people commented that it would soon become a tool for terrorists and black marketers. It would bring disaster to human civilization. Basically, it did not take much time for those experts to label the World Wide Web as a "doomsday tool."

In reality, many people tried to gauge the abilities of the World Wide Web but they failed miserably. Do you know why? It was growing at an exponential rate with every passing day. By now the World Wide Web has reached a state where we cannot even fathom the applications that it has and the ways it develops the internet. But one thing can be said for sure: the World Wide Web changed the way that the internet was viewed back then.

With the help of the web, the internet transformed from a potential tool of destruction to something useful on which the whole world depends today. In this decade, it is not even imaginable to live without access to the internet and the web; but we must never forget it was in the very same position once where Bitcoin is now.

**Actually, we human beings label everything that we do not fully understand as destructive or dangerous. It is our nature to try to understand the full extent of everything that we see or know. But when we fail, it does not take much time for us to label something dangerous.**

Many experts and enthusiasts have labeled Bitcoin as a threat to our socio-economic structure. But in reality, they have failed to understand the full extent of the abilities of Bitcoin. I have always said that money is the first application of Bitcoin. It is still growing and it still has a long way to go.

The truth is Bitcoin is a revolutionary technology and it will guide our current value system to its next stage.

Let's not forget that!

## 8.2. IS IT POSSIBLE TO COMPREHEND BITCOIN'S FULL ABILITIES?

As I have said before, it is not possible to understand the capabilities that Bitcoin possesses, similar to the internet. We have not yet been able to understand the full extent of the capabilities of the internet and we will never be able to do that. And from what we know so far, the same thing goes for Bitcoin.

**But the question is why it is not possible to measure the full range of capabilities of Bitcoin? Why have so many experts failed in doing so?**

The answer is actually very simple. The Bitcoin network is developing itself; it is growing at every single instance. The moment you try to understand the full set of capabilities it possesses, the Bitcoin network develops itself and it becomes impossible for you to grasp the range of its capabilities.

When we think very carefully, we can actually draw a beautiful parallel of Bitcoin with de Broglie's Uncertainty Principle, one of the most popular theories in particle physics. It states that the position and the velocity of an electron are not measurable at the same time.

Why is it so? Because whenever you try to measure the position of an electron its velocity changes and vice versa. The same thing goes for Bitcoin. Its structure is not static rather it is dynamic and it is continuously evolving or moving. Thus, there is practically no way of determining what it has to offer.

When you try to gauge the Bitcoin network, you are simply looking at the things that it can do at that point in time.

But when the capacity of the network or the load on the network increases, it gradually evolves the things that it can perform.

**"Wait, does that mean I can perform something with the Bitcoin network which I could not do earlier? Let's see what it can do now!"**

If this is the kind of question that is popping up at the back of your mind, then I must say that you will fail again miserably.

Even if you try to understand the extent of the capabilities of Bitcoin based on the data that you have received up until now, it will still not match as the moment you try to test it out, the network will have evolved further. Hence, it will never be possible to understand the capabilities of Bitcoin with pinpoint accuracy as it will always vary with time.

This is the thing that most of the people do not understand. They try to scale Bitcoin with what we know so far as a standard scale. But how will you standardize a network which evolves into something new with every passing minute? The fact is that people do not grasp this truth about Bitcoin, and so the arguments and debates are created.

Those who fail to understand this reality about Bitcoin argue about how it will fail miserably or the ways it will prove to be a disaster for everyone investing money in it.

As a matter of fact, at the very moment, there might be several individuals writing their doctoral dissertations on how Bitcoin will bring disaster. Though it may sound very funny, it is the very truth of our society. As I said earlier, we human beings love to label everything that we do not understand to its full extent as a threat.

To tell the truth, if I start a campaign in social media with the title "Bitcoin is still going strong," many people who have not kept track of this amazing technology will become dumbfounded.

"How can Bitcoin still be there? How is Bitcoin still going strong? How is it possible when we have been told years ago by these individuals with such and such degrees or designations that Bitcoin will fail miserably?"

This will be the reaction of many people. The fact is that those experts were proven wrong because it is impossible to understand the extent of Bitcoin's capabilities. And it will remain the same even three decades from now.

## 8.3. IS BITCOIN REALLY A CURSE FOR THE MODERN WORLD?

The fact that "every time we try to scale the capabilities of Bitcoin, we fail elegantly" will not change even in the years to come. Similarly, the arguments and debates on whether Bitcoin is a threat will never end. There is no stopping it.

These debates will continue until people accept the technology wholeheartedly and they start seeing it for what it is. That will happen once people realize the good that Bitcoin promises to do and how hopeless it is to gauge the capabilities of an ever-evolving network.

But every rumor that you hear about Bitcoin does not originate due to the fact that it is impossible to scale the Bitcoin network. Many institutions or people label Bitcoin as a disaster because it violates their interests. To be very honest, there are people with power and official designations who talk against this revolutionary technology because it goes against their interests.

**But who are these people and why are they doing so?**

The banks and financial institutions which are at the center of the corrupt value system at present are actually behind this. The decentralized network of Bitcoin has revolutionized the payment system, currency and above all the banking system completely.

The Bitcoin technology provides a network for the people only which promises to never become corrupted due to the centralization of power. The fact that Bitcoin offers these facilities is actually scaring the financial institutions. They are scared of losing their relevance in society; they are scared of losing the power. Thus, they resort to preaching to people about the disasters that Bitcoin will bring to the economy.

To be honest, none of this is a hoax; the financial institutions are scared about losing their relevance and it can be proved by the fact that the Chinese government has imposed a ban on Bitcoin exchanges and ICOs to limit Bitcoin transactions in the country.

This can be viewed as a planned effort to stop their banks from losing their relevance in their society. Despite these endless arguments and continuous efforts to prove Bitcoin a threat, the network is still thriving through all the adversities and it will continue to do so even in the future.

As I always say, Bitcoin is the future; it is the key to establishing a corruption-free value system and economy. And the day is not too far when Bitcoin will change the world completely and will guide us to the next stage.

**"[Bitcoin] is a remarkable cryptographic achievement... The ability to create something which is not duplicable in the digital world has enormous value...Lots of people will build businesses on top of that."** The executive chairman of Google, Erich Schmidt, said this about Bitcoin and there is no doubt that he was telling the very truth.

**Well, is Bitcoin really a threat?**

I leave it for you to answer!

# CHAPTER NINE

# BITCOIN VS. ALTCOINS

## What is Bitcoin?

Perhaps you can now provide a correct answer after all that we have discussed in the previous chapters.

However, if you are ever asked this question, the shortest answer that you can provide is: **"Bitcoin is a cryptocurrency which runs on blockchain technology."**

But here is the truth; Bitcoin is not the only cryptocurrency around! There are several others like Bitcoin which also use the blockchain network to complete their transactions. So, if you were thinking that Bitcoin was only the one of its kind, then you are wrong!

Though many people believe that the concept of cryptocurrency started with Bitcoin, there are several other systems that provide similar facilities and they are collectively called Altcoins or alternative cryptocurrencies.

**It makes you feel confused, right?**

**"Since the Altcoins exist, is it better to invest in Altcoins than Bitcoin? What should I do?"**

Probably, you are thinking all these and that is not going to get you anywhere.

Even though it is up to you to decide whether you want to invest in Altcoins rather than Bitcoin, I can show you which option is better and offers more promising aspects.

The debate about Bitcoin vs. Altcoins may not end anytime soon; but you will have the answer that you are looking for.

## 9.1. ALTCOINS: THE ALTERNATIVE CRYPTO-CURRENCIES

As I said before, the word "Altcoin" is used to describe all the alternatives of Bitcoin, that is, every other cryptocurrency available today.

There are hundreds of cryptocurrencies available today and every single one of them aims at replacing or improving Bitcoin in some way. Hence, the term Altcoin is well justified.

The Altcoins are not much different from Bitcoin. I have discussed with you the design and working of Bitcoin so you know how it works and you can understand how the Altcoins function.

Nevertheless, these alternative cryptocurrencies are not the exact mirror images of Bitcoin. They differ in some minor features like the speed of transaction and hashing or the method of distribution. I told you that the main goal of every single one of these Altcoins is to improve the Bitcoin network or to replace it; thus by changing small features, they try to outsmart the Bitcoin network.

But there is a major problem with the Altcoins. They do not last long except for a few such as Litecoin which has been around for quite some time now. Still, there are few Altcoins including Iota, Neo, Monero, Vertcoin and others that are improving rapidly without competing with Bitcoin. These systems are creating new horizons for investors.

Most Bitcoin investors, as well as enthusiasts, do not have high regard for the Altcoins and the point that they highlight is not quite legit. The infrastructure and the network that Bitcoin boasts is something that cannot be rivaled by the Altcoins. Well, that is true! But there are some Altcoins which offer even loftier prospects than Bitcoin.

## 9.1.1. Popular Altcoins: Cryptocurrencies that show a lot of promise

The decentralized but robust network of Bitcoin has truly revolutionized the monetary system today. The idea that was published in an excellent thesis paper in 2008 by someone under the pseudonym Satoshi Nakamoto has created a network that is redefining currency in a whole new way.

The decentralized network and blockchain technology have waged a war against the corrupt banking and payment system and slowly are disrupting it for the greater good. Almost a decade after its inception, Bitcoin has become a thing of legend and it has offered the people across the world a stable platform to invest in.

Naturally, Bitcoin has drawn a lot of attention to itself which has inspired development of several alternative cryptocurrencies or Altcoins. Since the creation of Namecoin in 2011, several Altcoins have surfaced. However, most of these alternate cryptocurrencies have been lost with the advent of time.

Thus, they failed to serve the one purpose for which they were built: providing a good challenge to Bitcoin. Yet there are several others which have survived the glare of time and have established themselves as the true competitors of Bitcoin.

**Let us have a look at these chief competitors of Bitcoin.**

### 9.1.2. Ethereum

When it comes to the most serious competitor of Bitcoin, there is no other cryptocurrency other than Ethereum that I can think of. Actually, if I had to choose the one Altcoin that comes with most promising features, then I would definitely choose Ethereum.

Ethereum was developed by VitalikButerin to compete with Bitcoin. It has truly become the fiercest rival that Bitcoin has ever had. Ethereum offers some new features which are not offered by the Bitcoin network.

Unlike Bitcoin, Ethereum binds all the agreements into the blockchain ledger itself with the help of its smart contract feature.

Feeling confused? It means Ethereum offers a better hashing algorithm than Bitcoin which in turn improves its speed of transaction.

Since it also runs on a blockchain network, Ethereum offers a decentralized network and it has truly proven itself to be a great investment platform. Above all, you can also use Ethereum currency to transact money to any part of the world just like BTC.

Having said all this, I must tell you that there is still a long way to go for Ethereum before it catches up with Bitcoin and there is no certainty that it will ever happen. However, if there is one cryptocurrency that has come closest to challenging the vast empire that Bitcoin has created, it's Ethereum.

Honestly, Ethereum provides new dimensions to the word "Altcoins" and there is no doubt about that.

### 9.1.3. Litecoin

Litecoin is one of the oldest Altcoins available in the market. It has been around for several years now and it has survived through all the ups and downs of the volatile cryptocurrency market.

Litecoin was created by a former Google engineer to improve the network of Bitcoin. The thing that is unique to Litecoin is its speed of creating a new block, and it is much faster than that of Bitcoin. As a result, Litecoin boasts much faster transactions.

However, when it comes to the infrastructure, it does not even come close to what Bitcoin offers. But this Altcoin has survived in this market and it is safe to say that Litecoin is here to stay. As a matter of fact, its value has increased with the increase in the value of Bitcoin. So, it is a competitor of Bitcoin and there is no wondering about that!

### 9.1.4. Lisk

Originally, Lisk started as a fork for Crypti but eventually, it developed into an amazing Altcoin. So, what is Lisk? Lisk is basically a blockchain application platform having its very own blockchain protocol. But the most interesting thing about Lisk is perhaps the consensus algorithm that it uses. Lisk uses Delegated Proof-Of-Stake (DPoS) consensus algorithm which is a much better, faster and improved version of Bitcoin's consensus mechanism. As a result, it takes much less time to do a transaction in Lisk.

Plus, it is one of those Altcoins that show immense promise even without competing with Bitcoin. Even though its price is much less compared to that of Bitcoin, its growth curve is far more impressive than what Bitcoin has. So, it is really one of those Altcoins worth having your eye on.

## 9.2. BITCOIN OR ALTCOINS: THE BEST PLACE FOR INVESTING

Now I have given you a proper idea of what Altcoins are, how they work and some of the most popular Altcoins that exist in the market today.

It is time for me to answer the ultimate question. It is time to settle the Bitcoin vs. Altcoin debate once and for all.

Before going into this debate, let me make one thing very clear to you. It has to be your decision ultimately; you will have to choose whether you need to invest in Bitcoin or Altcoins. Therefore, from here on, try to understand everything that I say very clearly.

I have told you that volatility exists everywhere you can invest. It is a risk that comes with every investment market. However, it is the duty of every investor to find the mode of investment which is less volatile and offers a great stability. This is the main point of investing money in any platform.

And this is where Bitcoin outsmarts the Altcoins. The stability and assurance of growth that Bitcoin offers cannot be matched by any other cryptocurrency.

### But the question is why? Why are the Altcoins so volatile?

The Altcoins are volatile because they have very small market capital. It means the market capital of each of these Altcoins is much less when compared to the market capital of Bitcoin. As a result, these cryptocurrencies are vulnerable to price manipulation by wealthy traders.

We generally call these traders "whales" because they often invest a humongous amount of money in the smaller cryptocurrencies to build hype. The aim behind this massive amount of fund injection is very hideous. These wealthy traders manipulate people to invest in the Altcoins by increasing their price greatly.

When the price increases greatly due to large-scale investments from a myriad of people, these whales sell their coins and withdraw their money from the market. They end up doubling the money that they had previously invested as profits.

## What happens when these whales withdraw their money all at once from the cryptocurrency?

The bubble bursts! As a result, the price of the coin falls drastically and the market crashes. In other words, you lose a great amount of money on your investments. This volatility that exists in the Altcoins market cannot be overlooked and it makes them very risky.

My point is that the volatility of the Altcoins market is something that cannot be trusted. Even if you are an experienced trader, you cannot predict with certainty what will be the fate of your investment tomorrow. However, this volatility is what makes the Altcoins so interesting. It gives you a great chance to get more out of your investments.

## But what is the deal with Bitcoin? How has it performed?

Honestly, Bitcoin has performed excellently. It is true that the Bitcoin market has gone through ups and downs but it has maintained a stability which is very unlikely for any investment platform.

## How has Bitcoin managed to remain stable?

The answer is very simple indeed. The market value of BTC is humongous and there are several traders across the world investing in Bitcoin every day. So, manipulating the price of Bitcoin is something that no one can ever achieve.

The reason that Bitcoin is trusted by millions of people across the globe is its infrastructure.

There are several economists and other experts warning people about Bitcoin. I have even seen people commenting on social media that the bubble of Bitcoin will soon burst.

Well, I have got news for you. It will never!

There are hundreds of cryptocurrencies available today and there will be several others in the future, but Bitcoin will never cease to exist. It will always be there at the top because it is the best in every aspect.

As of today, Bitcoin is considered the sixth largest currency in the world and it has taken the value system to a new dimension. So, the stability and prospects that Bitcoin offers cannot be matched by any alternative. Still, we cannot overlook the bright prospects that Altcoins offer.

**"Well, I think it is working. There may be other currencies like it that may be even better. But in the meantime, there's a big industry around Bitcoin. People have made fortunes off Bitcoin, some have lost money. It is volatile, but people make money off of volatility too."**– *Richard Branson*, founder of Virgin Galactic

The quote above is the proof of the effect that Bitcoin has on society; the way it inspires people across the world. No matter how many new Altcoins are created, they will never reach the same heights as Bitcoin.

As I said, whether you want to invest in Bitcoin or any other cryptocurrency is entirely your decision; but if you are looking for stability with an assured promise of great returns, then Bitcoin is the ideal choice.

The Bitcoin vs. Altcoin debate may never end, but you know who the winner is.

Don't you?

# CHAPTER TEN

# EXTRAORDINARY ALTCOINS – TAKING AHEAD THE LEGACY OF BITCOINS

I already have talked about Altcoins. And you probably know by now how significant they are on the map of the cryptocurrency world.

However, there are still several misconceptions prevalent even among top-notch cryptocurrency enthusiasts regarding Altcoins. Now we are going to break those misconceptions and understand the significance of Altcoins.

## So, what are Altcoins?

Let us brush up on the basics.

Altcoins are often portrayed as alternatives to Bitcoin; however, that is not always entirely true. Of course, Altcoins are inspired by the infrastructure of Bitcoin and they do not even come close to Bitcoin in terms of market capitalization as well as stability.

Yet there are a few important Altcoins that have made the decentralized blockchain technology their own and have taken it to new heights. Obviously, they cannot be compared to Bitcoin as of now; still, they show a promising growth rate and are destined for greatness.

I have said from the beginning that Bitcoin is just the first implementation of the amazing technology known as blockchain. Of course, Bitcoin helped us to put our faith in cryptocurrency and it made us believe that a decentralized payment or banking system is possible.

Actually, it gave us a glimpse of the future! And Bitcoin is still going strong and reaching new heights as I write. Still, I cannot say that the Bitcoin network is free of blemishes as that would be a lie. The consensus algorithm, transaction time and several such things can be improved. That is what Altcoins try to improve.

They are not some silly Bitcoin rip-off. They took the blockchain technology and made it their own. Altcoins actually are taking forward the huge legacy that Bitcoin has created. It is true that not every Altcoin is excellent and shows huge promise. Plus, volatility, whaling and several other problems exist in this market due to their small market capitalization.

On the other hand, it is also true that these factors do not apply to all Altcoins. There are a few Altcoins which are prospering even without competing with Bitcoin and making a respectable market hold for themselves.

And we are going to talk about them!

## 10.1. IOTA

Here, we have our first amazing Altcoin and it goes by the name of IOTA.

## So, what is Iota?

Well, it is better to say that it is actually the future of cryptocurrency. Why am I saying that?

IOTA is more than just a cryptocurrency; it is better to say that it is a futuristic protocol based on the distributed ledger. If I view IOTA from the perspective of a cryptocurrency then I can definitely say that it will blow your mind.

The best thing about IOTA is perhaps the functionalities that it offers. With its ability to do nano-transactions, unlimited scalability, zero transaction fees and quantum resistance, IOTA has overcome the limitations of a traditional cryptocurrency like Bitcoin.

Now, I have said before that transaction fees, low speed of transaction and low scalability are a few problems that every Bitcoin user faces. But here we are with an Altcoin that has overcome those limitations and is paving our way to the future.

## Wait! Isn't IOTA the Greek letter *i* that is used in problems of complex numbers?

Well, no! IOTA is anything other than complex. Having been born in 2014, it is the only cryptocurrency that acts as a futuristic distributed ledger with unlimited scalability, zero transaction fees, decentralization and quantum resistance.

IOTA is a currency that is perfect for the Internet of Things (IoT) and thus it is perfect for our daily lives.

In case it is new to you, IoT are the everyday items that are displayed on the internet or connected to the internet. Whether you are buying clothing online or booking a plane or train ticket, all of these are actually termed as the Internet of Things or IoT.

Now, the greatest problem with traditional cryptocurrencies like Bitcoin is their transaction fee. If you are trying to buy a movie ticket using Bitcoin then the transaction fees alone will exceed the cost of your ticket. Furthermore, nano-transactions are not possible in Bitcoin. Thus, these cryptocurrencies are basically unviable in the case of IoTs. That's why IOTA was created: so that it can fit perfectly into the scenario of our daily lives.

It is believed that in the future the paper currencies and plastic cards will be completely replaced by cryptocurrencies. However, that cannot happen unless the currency allows nano- or micropayments to become viable for the internet of things. That was actually the big idea behind creating this Altcoin.

IOTA works on an incredible technology called Tangle which is described as a data acrylic graph or DAG. This unique architecture is by far superior to the blockchain technology that Bitcoin uses. Thus, it has been able to overcome several limitations that blockchain technology has. Even if it is a non-blockchain cryptocurrency, it is still decentralized.

As of now, IOTA is one of the largest cryptocurrencies in the world and it continues to grow as well as to amaze people.

## 10.2. NEO

Well, NEO is just as amazing as Neo from *The Matrix* trilogy.

Actually, it has been one of the best cryptocurrencies of 2017 and it is still growing strong.

NEO is often called the Ethereum of China since it has become Ethereum's greatest competitor.

But let's not go there, rather let's focus on how promising the prospects of NEO are.

Neo is a cryptocurrency based on blockchain technology and it is the first decentralized currency that has been developed in China. Neo uses digital certificates to protect its transactions from any mishap. Neo was incepted in 2014 with the goal of easing the operation of trade and commerce.

To understand how NEO works, you must have an idea of the working of Ethereum as they are very similar. It uses digital assets and a smart contract platform like Ethereum on top of decentralized blockchain technology to perform transactions. So, it is fair to say that the transaction speed of NEO is much faster than that of Bitcoin.

As of now, NEO is one of the top cryptocurrencies in the world. And what is more interesting is the fact that it has maintained a stable growth curve for a long time now which is mostly unseen in the Altcoins market. With a fairly large market capitalization, NEO continues to grow stronger every hour and it helps everyone to hope for a better future without directly competing with Bitcoin.

## 10.3. MONERO

Monero was launched back in 2014 as the first private, secure and untraceable cryptocurrency in the world.

Yes, all of it's true and it is truly what it claims to be.

Though there are many who think that Monero is a private and more secure version of Bitcoin, that is not true at all. It is not a clone of Bitcoin rather it is a unique cryptocurrency that has been developed from scratch. The developers of Monero took blockchain technology and developed it in their own way to give birth to this amazing Altcoin.

### So, what makes Monero special?

As I said before, the functionalities that Monero offers help it to stand above the crowd. First, this Altcoin is absolutely private. No one will ever be able to check the balance that you have on your Monero wallet. No matter how extensively anyone searches the blockchain, they will never be able to see your balance due to the finest encryptions that this Altcoin uses.

Second, Monero is completely secure and untraceable. Yes, it is impossible to trace back a transaction to your account due to the irreversible mathematical equations that Monero uses in order to transact. This also gives the cryptocurrency unrivaled security. Security is a big issue in the world of Altcoins but with Monero, you will never have to worry about anything.

It goes without saying that the Monero blockchain is completely decentralized. Finally, the thing that really makes Monero a special Altcoin is the fact that it is totally fungible. What does that mean? It means that all the coins have the same value irrespective of the time and place.

Public transactions are a great problem for Bitcoin, and Monero is the answer to that problem. It focuses on anonymity and secures your wallet from every hacker on the planet.

Also, Monero has a large market capitalization and it has shown a stable growth over the course of time. And as per a recent market analysis, the figures will only continue to grow. So, if you are looking for anonymity for the investments you make, apart from all the brilliant investment prospects that it offers, Monero is one Altcoin that you need to look out for.

## 10.4. CARDANO (ADA)

CARDANO (ADA) is a unique cryptocurrency that has been developed by three organizations. The CARDANO Foundation, IOHK and Emurgo developed this cryptocurrency as a joint collaboration.

CARDANO was just launched on September 29, 2017, after two years of intensive research and development. Yet it has already become one of the top fifteen cryptocurrencies in the world.

It is also the first blockchain-based cryptocurrency that embarked on a scientific philosophy and research-driven approach for its development. The developers of CARDANO considered the interests of the users above all. Thus, they made CARDANO flexible and scalable as well as secure, so that millions of users can benefit from it.

CARDANO was developed on a smart contract platform like NEO and Ethereum. However, its developers claim that it has more advanced features than any other cryptocurrency that works on the smart contract platform. Furthermore, it is the first cryptocurrency to have used the Haskell Code, an industrial-strength language, for its development. Therefore, it is better to say that it has a highly robust infrastructure.

However, the most interesting thing about CARDANO is perhaps its use of an innovative consensus algorithm called Ouroboros. Thus, the transaction speed is much higher than most of the other cryptocurrencies including Bitcoin.

The fact that it has already become one of the largest cryptocurrencies in the market just a few months after its release actually shows how significant it is. Though it is not in competition with Bitcoin, it is still growing at a fast pace and is slowly becoming one of the trusted investment hubs for people.

## 10.5. GROESTLCOIN

Groestlcoin was one of the early birds in the Altcoin market as it has been around since early 2014. But what makes this Altcoin so special is that it has survived the competitive market and it is still going strong.

Like every traditional Altcoin, this currency also decentralized blockchain technology. The thing that makes it different lies in its consensus or Proof of Work (POW) mechanism. Before Groestlcoin, the consensus mechanism used by the cryptocurrencies was very slow. Thus, it resulted in very low transaction speed as it is the case for Bitcoin. However, the POW mechanism of this Altcoin is much less time-consuming, much more secure and above all less complex.

Furthermore, mining is one of the great aspects of cryptocurrency and it usually requires very expensive hardware as well as a great deal of time to mine the cryptocurrencies like Bitcoin. That is not applicable for Groestlcoin. It can also be mined in an old CPU unit without any hassle and it actually consumes much less time.

Above all, Groestlcoin is highly secured and it also maintains the anonymity of the users to a great extent. Even though it does not have huge market capitalization like Bitcoin, it is still a very large cryptocurrency. More importantly, Groestlcoin has a stable growth curve which even exceeds that of Bitcoin.

So, it is really a significant Altcoin that you must have your eye on.

I wonder why!

## 10.6. VERTCOIN

Vertcoin claims to be a "people's coin" since it allows peer-to-peer transactions similar to that of Bitcoin. The unique thing about this blockchain-powered decentralized currency is that it is owned as well as regulated by the users. There is no mining hardware or big organization behind Vertcoin. Rather, it can be mined by anyone to earn a profit.

As a matter of fact, Vertcoin was not developed by any organization but rather by the community members who provided time as volunteers. Furthermore, there is no ICO or airdrop for this Altcoin since it works entirely on donations and voluntary efforts. Why is there no ICO for Vertcoin? It was done by the developers in order to ensure a fair distribution of the Altcoin.

Vertcoin has unique software that can run on all operating systems as a multiplatform currency. However, the most interesting thing about the Vertcoin network is its ability to resist centralization completely.

Thus, it does not allow mining farms to mine the coins for their users. So, the issue of monopolizing the mining functionality will never be a problem for Vertcoin. Monopolizing the mining of the coins is a great problem that Bitcoin faces; thus it is one of those areas where Vertcoin is better than Bitcoin.

As far as market capitalization is concerned, I can assure you that it does not even come close to that of Bitcoin. Still, Vertcoin has witnessed steady growth over the years and it has proven itself as one of the most significant Altcoins in the market.

## 10.7. DASH

Of course, it would be not fair to leave Dash off my list. It has been one of the significant Altcoins since January 2014 and it is still booming.

Dash was created on January 18, 2014, by a developer named Evan Duffield, a supporter of making cryptocurrency transactions much more private. However, his ideas did not gain much support among the Bitcoin core developers. So he created a brand-new cryptocurrency using the core code of Bitcoin and several other new features.

Though the Altcoin was called Darkcoin in its early days, it was rebranded in February 2015 and was given the name Dash. Dash claims to be a peer-to-peer decentralized currency and it offers high liquidity like the real cash we have in different countries.

It is true that Dash uses the core code of Bitcoin, but it has two major improvements. First, the transactions in Dash are much more private as well as secured. Privacy of the transactions in Bitcoin is a big issue and Duffield made sure that his version of cryptocurrency is much more anonymous. Furthermore, the transactions are much faster in Dash as compared to Bitcoin. The proof of stake or POS mechanism that Dash uses is much more advanced, thus it takes very little time to transact the money.

Nonetheless, the unique thing about Dash is perhaps the fact that it has negligible transaction fees. You already know that transaction fees are a big issue for Bitcoin. But it seems that the developer team behind Dash found a way to curtail the fees to make them almost negligible.

Dash has a very large market capitalization and over the years it has proven itself to be a worthy successor of Bitcoin's legacy. With an incredible growth rate, Dash offers a great investment opportunity for people across the world.

## 10.8. FINAL WORDS

Altcoins are neither the replacement for Bitcoin nor are they a competitor. It is not possible for Altcoins to replace Bitcoin because the infrastructure that BTC offers cannot be rivaled. So, it is better to see the Altcoins as the successors of the legacy of the Bitcoin and that they are taking it forward to create a safe, uncorrupted and transparent payment or monetary environment for people across the world.

I have always said that Bitcoin is the revolution which is changing the failing value system that we have. And now you can comprehend the truth behind what I said. Bitcoin has inspired and is still inspiring developers across the globe to take aspects from it to create a much better currency of their own.

Altcoins are significant and they offer great prospects in terms of the payment system and transactions as well as investments. They do not have to compete with Bitcoin but with their more advanced functionalities they are helping to create a stronghold for themselves in the world of Bitcoin.

**"I am very excited about the prospect of using cryptocurrency, not just as a money equivalent, but using it as a way to earn something as a result of doing some type of work."** – *William Mougayar*, co-author of *The Business Blockchain*

The quote above perfectly defines how I feel about Altcoins and cryptocurrency.

It does not matter whether it is more profitable to invest in Bitcoin or Altcoins. The thing that matters most is the fact that the development of Altcoins creates infinite opportunities for the future.

As a technology, Bitcoin is surely legendary and groundbreaking but as I said before it has its own flaws. Similarly, these Altcoins try to get rid of those flaws in their design yet they are not flawless themselves. This leaves room for more research and experimentation to develop the ultimate currency for the people. And that is the future I am rooting for.

To an everyday person's eye, Altcoins may not have much significance since they do not possess the market capitalization or the high value of Bitcoin. But I have always said to see the cryptocurrencies from the perspective of technology. If you do that then you will understand why it is so exciting.

# FAQs ON BITCOIN

### 1) What is Bitcoin?

Bitcoin is a consensus network that enables a new payment system and a completely digital money. It is the first decentralized peer-to-peer payment network that is powered by its users with no central authority or middlemen. From a user perspective, Bitcoin is pretty much like cash for the Internet. Bitcoin also can be seen as the most prominent triple entry bookkeeping system in existence.

### 2) Who created Bitcoin?

Bitcoin is the first implementation of a concept called "cryptocurrency" which was first described in 1998 by Wei Dai on the cypherpunks mailing list, suggesting the idea of a new form of money that uses cryptography to control its creation and transactions, rather than a central authority. The first Bitcoin specification and proof of concept was published in 2009 in a cryptography mailing list by Satoshi Nakamoto. Satoshi left the project in late 2010 without revealing much about himself. The community has since grown exponentially with many developers working on Bitcoin.

Satoshi's anonymity often raised unjustified concerns, many of which are linked to misunderstanding of the open-source nature of Bitcoin. The Bitcoin protocol and software are published openly and any developers around the world can review the code or make their own modified version of the Bitcoin software. Just like current developers, Satoshi's influence was limited to the changes he made being adopted by others and therefore he did not control Bitcoin. As such, the identity of Bitcoin's inventor is probably as relevant today as the identity of the person who invented paper.

### 3) Who controls the Bitcoin network?

Nobody owns the Bitcoin network much like no one owns the technology behind email. Bitcoin is controlled by all Bitcoin users around the world. While developers are improving the software, they can't force a change in the Bitcoin protocol because all users are free to choose what software and version they use. In order to stay compatible with each other, all users need to use software complying with the same rules. Bitcoin can only work correctly with a complete consensus among all users. Therefore, all users and developers have a strong incentive to protect this consensus.

### 4) How does Bitcoin work?

From a user perspective, Bitcoin is nothing more than a mobile app or computer program that provides a personal Bitcoin wallet and allows a user to send and receive Bitcoins with them. This is how Bitcoin works for most users.

Behind the scenes, the Bitcoin network is sharing a public ledger called the blockchain. This ledger contains every transaction ever processed, allowing a user's computer to verify the validity of each transaction. The authenticity of each transaction is protected by digital signatures corresponding to the sending addresses, allowing all users to have full control over sending Bitcoins from their own Bitcoin addresses. In addition, anyone can process transactions using the computing power of specialized hardware and earn a reward in Bitcoins for this service. This is often called "mining." To learn more about Bitcoin, you can consult the dedicated page and the original paper.

### 5) Is Bitcoin really used by people?

Yes. There are a growing number of businesses and individuals using Bitcoin. This includes brick-and-mortar businesses like restaurants, apartments and law firms, as well as popular online services such as Namecheap, Overstock.com and Reddit. While Bitcoin remains a relatively new phenomenon, it is growing fast. At the end of April 2017, the total value of all existing Bitcoins exceeded $20 billion US, with millions of dollars' worth of Bitcoins exchanged daily.

### 6) How does one acquire Bitcoins?

- As payment for goods or services.
- By purchasing Bitcoins at a Bitcoin exchange.
- By exchanging Bitcoins with someone near you.
- By earning Bitcoins through competitive mining.

While it may be possible to find individuals who wish to sell Bitcoins through a credit card or PayPal payment, most exchanges do not allow funding via these payment methods. This is due to cases where someone buys Bitcoins with PayPal and then reverses their half of the transaction. This is commonly referred to as a chargeback.

### 7) How difficult is it to make a Bitcoin payment?

Bitcoin payments are easier to make than debit or credit card purchases, and they can be received without a merchant account. Payments are made from a wallet application, either on your computer or smartphone, by entering the recipient's address and payment amount, and pressing send. To make it easier to enter a recipient's address, many wallets can obtain the address by scanning a QR code or touching two phones together with NFC technology.

### 8) What are the advantages of Bitcoin?

- **Payment freedom:** It is possible to send and receive Bitcoins anywhere in the world at any time. No bank holidays. No borders. No bureaucracy. Bitcoin allows its users to be in full control of their money.
- **Choose your own fees:** There is no fee to receive Bitcoins, and many wallets let you control how

large a fee to pay when spending. Higher fees can encouragefaster confirmation of your transactions. Fees are unrelated to the amount transferred, so it's possible to send 100,000 Bitcoins for the same fee it costs to send 1 Bitcoin. Additionally, merchant processors exist to assist merchants in processing transactions, converting Bitcoins to fiat currency and depositing funds directly into merchants' bank accounts daily. As these services are based on Bitcoin, they can be offered for much lower fees than with PayPal or credit card networks.

- **Fewer risks for merchants:** Bitcoin transactions are secure, irreversible, and do not contain customers' sensitive or personal information. This protects merchants from losses caused by fraud or fraudulent chargebacks, and there is no need for PCI compliance. Merchants can easily expand to new markets where credit cards are not available or fraud rates are unacceptably high. The net results are lower fees, larger markets and fewer administrative costs.

- **Security and control:** Bitcoin users are in full control of their transactions; it is impossible for merchants to force unwanted or unnoticed charges as can happen with other payment methods. Bitcoin payments can be made without personal information tied to the transaction. This offers strong protection against identity theft. Bitcoin users can also protect their money with backup and encryption.

- **Transparency and neutrality:** All information concerning the Bitcoin money supply itself is readily available on the blockchain for anybody to verify and use in real-time. No individual or organization can control or manipulate the Bitcoin protocol because it is cryptographically secure. This allows the core of Bitcoin to be trusted for being completely neutral, transparent and predictable.

## 9) What are the disadvantages of Bitcoin?

- **Degree of acceptance:** Many people are still unaware of Bitcoin. Every day, more businesses accept Bitcoins because they want the advantages of doing so, but the list remains small and still needs to grow in order to benefit from network effects.

- **Volatility:** The total value of Bitcoins in circulation and the number of businesses using Bitcoin are still very small compared to what they could be. Therefore, relatively small events, trades or business activities can significantly affect the price. In theory, this volatility will decrease as Bitcoin markets and technology mature. Never before has the world seen a start-up currency, so it is truly difficult (and exciting) to imagine how it will play out.

- **Ongoing development:** Bitcoin software is still in beta with many incomplete features in active development. New tools, features and services are being developed to make Bitcoin more secure and accessible to the masses. Some of these are still not ready for everyone. Most Bitcoin businesses are new and still offer no insurance. In general, Bitcoin is still in the process of maturing.

## 10) Why do people trust Bitcoin?

Much of the trust in Bitcoin comes from the fact that it requires no trust at all. Bitcoin is fully open-source and decentralized. This means that anyone has access to the entire source code at any time. Any developer in the world can therefore verify exactly how Bitcoin works. All transactions and Bitcoins issued into existence can be transparently consulted in real-time by anyone. All payments can be made without reliance on a third party and the whole system is protected by heavily peer-reviewed cryptographic algorithms like those used for online banking. No organization or individual can control Bitcoin, and the network remains secure even if not all of its users can be trusted.

### 11) Can I make money with Bitcoin?

You should never expect to get rich with Bitcoin or any emerging technology. It is always important to be wary of anything that sounds too good to be true or disobeys basic economic rules.

Bitcoin is a growing space of innovation and there are business opportunities that also include risks. There is no guarantee that Bitcoin will continue to grow even though it has developed at a very fast rate so far. Investing time and resources on anything related to Bitcoin requires entrepreneurship. There are various ways to make money with Bitcoin such as mining, speculation or running new businesses. All these methods are competitive and there is no guarantee of profit. It is up to each individual to make a proper evaluation of the costs and the risks involved in any such project.

### 12) Is Bitcoin fully virtual and immaterial?

Bitcoin is as virtual as the credit cards and online banking networks people use every day. Bitcoin can be used to pay online and in physical stores just like any other form of money. Bitcoins can also be exchanged in physical form such as the Denarium coins, but paying with a mobile phone usually remains more convenient. Bitcoin balances are stored in a large distributed network, and they cannot be fraudulently altered by anybody. In other words, Bitcoin users have exclusive control over their funds and Bitcoins cannot vanish just because they are virtual.

### 13) Is Bitcoin anonymous?

Bitcoin is designed to allow its users to send and receive payments with an acceptable level of privacy. However, Bitcoin is not anonymous and cannot offer the same level of privacy as cash. The use of Bitcoin leaves extensive public records. Various mechanisms exist to protect users' privacy, and more are in development. However, there is still work to be done before these features are used correctly by most Bitcoin users.

Some concerns have been raised that private transactions could be used for illegal purposes with Bitcoin. However, it is worth noting that Bitcoin will undoubtedly be subjected to similar regulations that are already in place inside existing financial systems. Bitcoin cannot be more anonymous than cash and it is not likely to prevent criminal investigations from being conducted. Additionally, Bitcoin is also designed to prevent a large range of financial crimes.

**14) What happens when Bitcoins are lost?**

When a user loses a wallet, it has the effect of removing money out of circulation. Lost Bitcoins still remain in the blockchain just like any other Bitcoins. However, lost Bitcoins remain dormant forever because there is no way for anybody to find the private key(s) that would allow them to be spent again. Because of the law of supply and demand, when fewer Bitcoins are available, the ones that are left will be in higher demand and increase in value to compensate.

**15) Can Bitcoin scale to become a major payment network?**

The Bitcoin network can already process a much higher number of transactions per second than it does today. It is, however, not entirely ready to scale to the level of major credit card networks. Work is underway to lift current limitations, and future requirements are well known. Since inception, every aspect of the Bitcoin network has been in a continuous process of maturation, optimization and specialization, and it should be expected to remain that way for some years to come. As traffic grows, more Bitcoin users may use lightweight clients, and full network nodes may become a more specialized service.

### 16) Is Bitcoin legal?

To the best of our knowledge, Bitcoin has not been made illegal by legislation in most jurisdictions. However, some jurisdictions (such as Argentina and Russia) severely restrict or ban foreign currencies. Other jurisdictions (such as Thailand) may limit the licensing of certain entities such as Bitcoin exchanges.

Regulators from various jurisdictions are taking steps to provide individuals and businesses with rules on how to integrate this new technology with the formal, regulated financial system. For example, the Financial Crimes Enforcement Network (FinCEN), a bureau in the United States Treasury Department, issued non-binding guidance on how it characterizes certain activities involving virtual currencies.

### 17) Is Bitcoin useful for illegal activities?

Bitcoin is money, and money has always been used both for legal and illegal purposes. Cash, credit cards and current banking systems widely surpass Bitcoin in terms of their use to finance crime. Bitcoin can bring significant innovation in payment systems and the benefits of such innovation are often considered to be far beyond their potential drawbacks.

Bitcoin is designed to be a huge step forward in making money more secure and could also act as a significant protection against many forms of financial crime. For instance, Bitcoins are completely impossible to counterfeit. Users are in full control of their payments and cannot receive unapproved charges such as with credit card fraud. Bitcoin transactions are irreversible and immune to fraudulent chargebacks. Bitcoin allows money to be secured against theft and loss using very strong and useful mechanisms such as backups, encryption and multiple signatures.

Some concerns have been raised that Bitcoin could be more attractive to criminals because it can be used to make private and irreversible payments. However, these features already exist with cash and wire transfer, which are widely used and well-established. The use of Bitcoin will undoubtedly be subjected to similar regulations that are already in place inside existing financial systems, and Bitcoin is not likely to prevent criminal investigations from being conducted. In general, it is common for important breakthroughs to be perceived as being controversial before their benefits are well understood. The internet is a good example among many others to illustrate this.

## 18) Can Bitcoin be regulated?

The Bitcoin protocol itself cannot be modified without the cooperation of nearly all its users, who choose what software they use. Attempting to assign special rights to a local authority in the rules of the global Bitcoin network is not a practical possibility. Any rich organization could choose to invest in mining hardware to control half of the computing power of the network and become able to block or reverse recent transactions. However, there is no guarantee that they could retain this power since this requires investing more than all other miners in the world.

It is however possible to regulate the use of Bitcoin in a similar way to any other instrument. Just like the dollar, Bitcoin can be used for a wide variety of purposes, some of which can be considered legitimate or not as per each jurisdiction's laws. In this regard, Bitcoin is no different than any other tool or resource and can be subjected to different regulations in each country. Bitcoin use could also be made difficult by restrictive regulations, in which case it is hard to determine what percentage of users would keep using the technology. A government that chooses to ban Bitcoin would prevent domestic businesses and markets from developing, shifting innovation to other countries. The challenge for regulators, as always, is to develop efficient solutions while not impairing the growth of new emerging markets and businesses.

### 19) What about Bitcoin and taxes?

Bitcoin is not a fiat currency with legal tender status in any jurisdiction, but often tax liability accrues regardless of the medium used. There is a wide variety of legislation in many different jurisdictions which could cause income, sales, payroll, capital gains or some other form of tax liability to arise with Bitcoin.

### 20) What about Bitcoin and consumer protection?

Bitcoin is freeing people to transact on their own terms. Each user can send and receive payments in a similar way to cash but they can also take part in more complex contracts. Multiple signatures allow a transaction to be accepted by the network only if a certain number of a defined group of persons agree to sign the transaction. This allows innovative dispute mediation services to be developed in the future. Such services could allow a third party to approve or reject a transaction in case of disagreement between the other parties without having control on their money. As opposed to cash and other payment methods, Bitcoin always leaves a public proof that a transaction did take place, which can potentially be used in a recourse against businesses with fraudulent practices.

It is also worth noting that while merchants usually depend on their public reputation to remain in business and pay their employees, they don't have access to the same level of information when dealing with new consumers. The way Bitcoin works allows both individuals and businesses to be protected against fraudulent chargebacks while giving the choice to the consumers to ask for more protection when they are not willing to trust a particular merchant.

### 21) How are Bitcoins created?

New Bitcoins are generated by a competitive and decentralized process called "mining." This process involves the network rewarding individuals for their services.

Bitcoin miners are processing transactions and securing the network using specialized hardware and are collecting new Bitcoins in exchange.

The Bitcoin protocol is designed in such a way that new Bitcoins are created at a fixed rate. This makes Bitcoin mining a very competitive business. When more miners join the network, it becomes increasingly difficult to make a profit and miners must seek efficiency to cut their operating costs. No central authority or developer has any power to control or manipulate the system to increase their profits. Every Bitcoin node in the world will reject anything that does not comply with the rules it expects the system to follow.

Bitcoins are created at a decreasing and predictable rate. The number of new Bitcoins created each year is automatically halved over time until Bitcoin issuance halts completely with a total of 21 million Bitcoins in existence. At this point, Bitcoin miners will probably be supported exclusively by numerous small transaction fees.

### 22) Why do Bitcoins have value?

Bitcoins have value because they are useful as a form of money. Bitcoin has the characteristics of money (durability, portability, fungibility, scarcity, divisibility and recognizability) based on the properties of mathematics rather than relying on physical properties (like gold and silver) or trust in central authorities (like fiat currencies). In short, Bitcoin is backed by mathematics. With these attributes, all that is required for a form of money to hold value is trust and adoption. In the case of Bitcoin, this can be measured by its growing base of users, merchants and startups. As with all currency, Bitcoin's value comes only and directly from people willing to accept them as payment.

### 23) What determines Bitcoin's price?

The price of a Bitcoin is determined by supply and demand. When demand for Bitcoins increases, the price increases, and when demand falls, the price falls. There is only a limited number of Bitcoins in circulation and new Bitcoins are created at a predictable and decreasing rate, which means that demand must follow this level of inflation to keep the price stable. Because Bitcoin is still a relatively small market compared to what it could be, it doesn't take significant amounts of money to move the market price up or down, and thus the price of a Bitcoin is still very volatile.

## 24) Can Bitcoins become worthless?

Yes. History is littered with currencies that failed and are no longer used, such as the German mark during the Weimar Republic and, more recently, the Zimbabwean dollar. Although previous currency failures were typically due to hyperinflation of a kind that Bitcoin makes impossible, there is always potential for technical failures, competing currencies, political issues and so on. As a basic rule of thumb, no currency should be considered absolutely safe from failures or hard times. Bitcoin has proven reliable for years since its inception and there is a lot of potential for Bitcoin to continue to grow. However, no one is in a position to predict what the future will be for Bitcoin.

## 25) Is Bitcoin a bubble?

A fast rise in price does not constitute a bubble. An artificial over-valuation that will lead to a sudden downward correction constitutes a bubble. Choices based on individual human action by hundreds of thousands of market participants cause Bitcoin's price to fluctuate as the market seeks price discovery. Reasons for changes in sentiment may include a loss of confidence in Bitcoin, a large difference between value and price not based on the fundamentals of the Bitcoin economy, increased press coverage stimulating speculative demand, fear of uncertainty and old-fashioned irrational exuberance and greed.

## 26) Is Bitcoin a Ponzi scheme?

A Ponzi scheme is a fraudulent investment operation that pays returns to its investors from their own money, or the money paid by subsequent investors, instead of from profit earned by the individuals running the business. Ponzi schemes are designed to collapse at the expense of the last investors when there are not enough new participants.

Bitcoin is a free software project with no central authority. Consequently, no one is in a position to make fraudulent representations about investment returns. Like other major currencies such as gold, United States dollar, euro, yen, etc., there is no guaranteed purchasing power and the exchange rate floats freely. This leads to volatility where owners of bitcoins can unpredictably make or lose money. Beyond speculation, Bitcoin is also a payment system with useful and competitive attributes that are being used by thousands of users and businesses.

## 27) Doesn't Bitcoin unfairly benefit early adopters?

Some early adopters have large numbers of Bitcoins because they took risks and invested time and resources in an unproven technology that was hardly used by anyone and that was much harder to secure properly. Many early adopters spent large numbers of Bitcoins quite a few times before they became valuable or bought only small amounts and didn't make huge gains. There is no guarantee that the price of a Bitcoin will increase or drop. This is very similar to investing in an early startup that can either gain value through its usefulness and popularity, or just never break through. Bitcoin is still in its infancy, and it has been designed with a very long-term view; it is hard to imagine how it could be less biased towards early adopters, and today's users may or may not be the early adopters of tomorrow.

### 28) Won't the finite number of Bitcoins be a limitation?

Bitcoin is unique in that only 21 million Bitcoins will ever be created. However, this will never be a limitation because transactions can be denominated in smaller sub-units of a Bitcoin, such as bits – there are 1,000,000 bits in 1 Bitcoin. Bitcoins can be divided up to 8 decimal places (0.000 000 01) and potentially even smaller units if that is ever required in the future as the average transaction size decreases.

### 29) Won't Bitcoin fall in a deflationary spiral?

The deflationary spiral theory says that if prices are expected to fall, people will move purchases into the future to benefit from the lower prices. That fall in demand will in turn cause merchants to lower their prices to try and stimulate demand, making the problem worse and leading to an economic depression.

Although this theory is a popular way to justify inflation amongst central bankers, it does not appear to always hold true and is considered controversial amongst economists. Consumer electronics is one example of a market where prices constantly fall but which is not in depression. Similarly, the value of Bitcoins has risen over time and yet the size of the Bitcoin economy has also grown dramatically along with it. Because both the value of the currency and the size of its economy started at zero in 2009, Bitcoin is a counterexample to the theory showing that it must sometimes be wrong.

Notwithstanding this, Bitcoin is not designed to be a deflationary currency. It is more accurate to say Bitcoin is intended to inflate in its early years and become stable in its later years. The only time the quantity of Bitcoins in circulation will drop is if people carelessly lose their wallets by failing to make backups. With a stable monetary base and a stable economy, the value of the currency should remain the same.

### 30) Isn't speculation and volatility a problem for Bitcoin?

This is a chicken and egg situation. For Bitcoin's price to stabilize, a large-scale economy needs to develop with more businesses and users. For a large-scale economy to develop, businesses and users will seek price stability.

Fortunately, volatility does not affect the main benefits of Bitcoin as a payment system to transfer money from point A to point B. It is possible for businesses to convert Bitcoin payments to their local currency instantly, allowing them to profit from the advantages of Bitcoin without being subjected to price fluctuations. Since Bitcoin offers many useful and unique features and properties, many people choose to use Bitcoin. With such solutions and incentives, it is possible that Bitcoin will mature and develop to a degree where price volatility will become limited.

### 31) What if someone bought up all the existing Bitcoins?

Only a fraction of Bitcoins issued to date are found on the exchange markets for sale. Bitcoin markets are competitive, meaning the price of a Bitcoin will rise or fall depending on supply and demand. Additionally, new Bitcoins will continue to be issued for decades to come. Therefore even the most determined buyer could not buy all the Bitcoins in existence. This situation doesn't mean, however, that the markets aren't vulnerable to price manipulation; it still doesn't take significant amounts of money to move the market price up or down, and Bitcoin remains a volatile asset thus far.

### 32) What if someone creates a better digital currency?

That can happen. For now, Bitcoin remains by far the most popular decentralized virtual currency, but there can be no guarantee that it will retain that position. There is already a set of alternative currencies inspired by Bitcoin. It is however probably correct to assume that significant improvements would be required for a new currency to overtake Bitcoin in terms of established market, even though this remains unpredictable. Bitcoin could also conceivably adopt improvements of a competing currency so long as it doesn't change fundamental parts of the protocol.

### 33) Why do I have to wait for confirmation?

Receiving notification of a payment is almost instant with Bitcoin. However, there is a delay before the network begins to confirm your transaction by including it in a block. A confirmation means that there is a consensus on the network that the Bitcoins you received haven't been sent to anyone else and are considered your property. Once your transaction has been included in one block, it will continue to be buried under every block after it, which will exponentially consolidate this consensus and decrease the risk of a reversed transaction. Each confirmation takes between a few seconds and 90 minutes, with 10 minutes being the average. If the transaction pays too low a fee or is otherwise atypical, getting the first confirmation can take much longer. Every user is free to determine at what point they consider a transaction sufficiently confirmed, but 6 confirmations is often considered to be as safe as waiting 6 months on a credit card transaction.

### 34) How much will the transaction fee be?

Transactions can be processed without fees, but trying to send free transactions can require waiting days or weeks. Although fees may increase over time, normal fees currently only cost a tiny amount. By default, all Bitcoin wallets listed on Bitcoin.org add what they think is an appropriate fee to your transactions; most of those wallets will also give you chance to review the fee before sending the transaction.

Transaction fees are used as a protection against users sending transactions to overload the network and as a way to pay miners for their work helping to secure the network. The precise manner in which fees work is still being developed and will change over time. Because the fee is not related to the number of Bitcoins being sent, it may seem extremely low or unfairly high. Instead, the fee is relative to the number of bytes in the transaction, so using multisig or spending multiple previously received amounts may cost more than simpler transactions. If your activity follows the pattern of conventional transactions, you won't have to pay unusually high fees.

### 35) What if I receive a Bitcoin when my computer is powered off?

This works fine. The Bitcoins will appear next time you start your wallet application. Bitcoins are not actually received by the software on your computer, they are appended to a public ledger that is shared between all the devices on the network. If you are sent Bitcoins when your wallet client program is not running and you later launch it, it will download blocks and catch up with any transactions it did not already know about, and the Bitcoins will eventually appear as if they were just received in real time. Your wallet is only needed when you wish to spend Bitcoins.

### 36) What does "synchronizing" mean and why does it take so long?

Long synchronization time is only required with full node clients like Bitcoin Core. Technically speaking, synchronizing is the process of downloading and verifying all previous Bitcoin transactions on the network. For some Bitcoin clients to calculate the spendable balance of your Bitcoin wallet and make new transactions, the client need to be aware of all previous transactions. This step can be resource intensive and requires sufficient bandwidth and storage to accommodate the full size of the blockchain. For Bitcoin to remain secure, enough people should keep using full node clients because they perform the task of validating and relaying transactions.

### 37) What is Bitcoin mining?

Mining is the process of spending computing power to process transactions, secure the network and keep everyone in the system synchronized together. It can be perceived like the Bitcoin data center except that it has been designed to be fully decentralized with miners operating in all countries and no individual having control over the network. This process is referred to as "mining" as an analogy to gold mining because it is also a temporary mechanism used to issue new Bitcoins. Unlike gold mining, however, Bitcoin mining provides a reward in exchange for useful services required to operate a secure payment network. Mining will still be required after the last Bitcoin is issued.

### 38) How does Bitcoin mining work?

Anybody can become a Bitcoin miner by running software with specialized hardware. Mining software listens for transactions broadcast through the peer-to-peer network and performs appropriate tasks to process and confirm these transactions. Bitcoin miners perform this work because they can earn transaction fees, paid by users for faster transaction processing, and newly created Bitcoins issued into existence according to a fixed formula.

For new transactions to be confirmed, they need to be included in a block along with a mathematical proof of work. Such proofs are very hard to generate because there is no way to create them other than by trying billions of calculations per second. This requires miners to perform these calculations before their blocks are accepted by the network and before they are rewarded. As more people start to mine, the difficulty of finding valid blocks is automatically increased by the network to ensure that the average time to find a block remains equal to 10 minutes. As a result, mining is a very competitive business where no individual miner can control what is included in the blockchain.

The proof of work is also designed to depend on the previous block to force a chronological order in the blockchain. This makes it exponentially difficult to reverse previous transactions because this requires the recalculation of the proofs of work of all the subsequent blocks. When two blocks are found at the same time, miners work on the first block they receive and switch to the longest chain of blocks as soon as the next block is found. This allows mining to secure and maintain a global consensus based on processing power.

Bitcoin miners are neither able to cheat by increasing their own reward nor process fraudulent transactions that could corrupt the Bitcoin network because all Bitcoin nodes would reject any block that contains invalid data as per the rules of the Bitcoin protocol. Consequently, the network remains secure even if not all Bitcoin miners can be trusted.

### 39) Isn't Bitcoin mining a waste of energy?

Spending energy to secure and operate a payment system is hardly a waste. Like any other payment service, the use of Bitcoin entails processing costs. Services necessary for the operation of currently widespread monetary systems, such as banks, credit cards and armored vehicles, also use a lot of energy. Although unlike Bitcoin, their total energy consumption is not transparent and cannot be as easily measured.

Bitcoin mining has been designed to become more optimized over time with specialized hardware consuming less energy, and the operating costs of mining should continue to be proportional to demand. When Bitcoin mining becomes too competitive and less profitable, some miners choose to stop their activities. Furthermore, all energy expended mining is eventually transformed into heat, and the most profitable miners will be those who have put this heat to good use. An optimally efficient mining network is one that isn't actually consuming any extra energy. While this is an ideal, the economics of mining are such that miners individually strive toward it.

**40) How does mining help secure Bitcoin?**

Mining creates the equivalent of a competitive lottery that makes it very difficult for anyone to consecutively add new blocks of transactions into the blockchain. This protects the neutrality of the network by preventing any individual from gaining the power to block certain transactions. This also prevents any individuals from replacing parts of the blockchain to roll back their own spends, which could be used to defraud other users. Mining makes it exponentially more difficult to reverse a past transaction by requiring the rewriting of all blocks following this transaction.

**41) What do I need to start mining?**

In the early days of Bitcoin, anyone could find a new block using their computer's CPU. As more and more people started mining, the difficulty of finding new blocks increased greatly to the point where the only cost-effective method of mining today is using specialized hardware. You can visit BitcoinMining.com for more information

**42) Is Bitcoin secure?**

The Bitcoin technology – the protocol and the cryptography – has a strong security track record, and the Bitcoin network is probably the biggest distributed computing project in the world. Bitcoin's most common vulnerability is in user error. Bitcoin wallet files that store the necessary private keys can be accidentally deleted, lost or stolen. This is pretty similar to physical cash stored in a digital form. Fortunately, users can employ sound security practices to protect their money or use service providers that offer good levels of security and insurance against theft or loss.

## 43) Hasn't Bitcoin been hacked in the past?

The rules of the protocol and the cryptography used for Bitcoin are still working years after its inception, which is a good indication that the concept is well designed. However, security flaws have been found and fixed over time in various software implementations. Like any other form of software, the security of Bitcoin software depends on the speed with which problems are found and fixed. The more such issues are discovered, the more Bitcoin is gaining maturity.

There are often misconceptions about thefts and security breaches that happened on diverse exchanges and businesses. Although these events are unfortunate, none of them involve Bitcoin itself being hacked, nor imply inherent flaws in Bitcoin; just as a bank robbery doesn't mean that the dollar is compromised. However, it is accurate to say that a complete set of good practices and intuitive security solutions is needed to give users better protection of their money, and to reduce the general risk of theft and loss. Over the course of the last few years, such security features have quickly developed, such as wallet encryption, offline wallets, hardware wallets and multi-signature transactions.

## 44) Could users collude against Bitcoin?

It is not possible to change the Bitcoin protocol that easily. Any Bitcoin clients that don't comply with the same rules cannot enforce their own rules on other users. As per the current specification, double spending is not possible on the same blockchain, and neither is spending Bitcoins without a valid signature. Therefore, it is not possible to generate uncontrolled amounts of Bitcoins out of thin air, spend other users' funds, corrupt the network or anything similar.

However, powerful miners could arbitrarily choose to block or reverse recent transactions. A majority of users can also put pressure for some changes to be adopted. Because

Bitcoin only works correctly with a complete consensus between all users, changing the protocol can be very difficult and requires an overwhelming majority of users to adopt the changes in such a way that remaining users have nearly no choice but to follow. As a general rule, it is hard to imagine why any Bitcoin users would choose to adopt any change that could compromise their own money.

**45) Is Bitcoin vulnerable to quantum computing?**

Yes, most systems relying on cryptography in general are, including traditional banking systems. However, quantum computers don't yet exist and probably won't for a while. In the event that quantum computing could be an imminent threat to Bitcoin, the protocol could be upgraded to use post-quantum algorithms. Given the importance that this update would have, it can be safely expected that it would be highly reviewed by developers and adopted by all Bitcoin users.

**46) What is the blockchain?**

Bitcoin is dependent on the blockchain that underlies and structures the system. The blockchain is the vertebrae of the protocol and the glue that holds the network together. It is simply a vast, distributed public ledger of account. It keeps track of every transaction ever made in the network, and all transactions are timestamped and verified by network miners. This is how it works: miners with specialized computers compete to solve mathematical puzzles with other computers, and once they solve a puzzle they are awarded some Bitcoin, but they also add a "block" of completed transactions to the blockchain for future viewing and verifiability. Once a block is added to the chain, the cycle repeats itself, and the computers continue to compete to solve these difficult problems. Every transaction on the blockchain is completely transparent and accounted for in its log. Anyone can see the public keys of any transaction they want (although there are no names associated with transactions). One could go all the way back and view the very first transactions ever made on the first block ever created. This block was unironically called the Genesis Block.

## 47) How is the blockchain different from banking ledgers?

Banks and accounting systems use ledgers to track and timestamp transactions. The difference is that the blockchain is completely decentralized and open source. This means that people do not have to rely on or trust the central bank to keep track of the transactions. The peer-to-peer blockchain technology can keep track of all the transactions without the fear of having them erased or lost. Furthermore, the blockchain, because of its open source nature, is more versatile and programmable than central banking ledgers. If programmers need new functionality on the blockchain, they can simply innovate on top of already existing software through consensus. This is difficult for central banks because of all their regulations and central points of failure.

## 48) What is a private blockchain?

Private blockchains are deployed either within an organization or shared among a known group of participants. They can be limited to a predefined set of participants. In this case, no one else can access them or the data residing in them. They can be secured in a similar way to securing other integrated enterprise applications (such as firewalls, VPN, etc.).

## 49) What Is a smart contract?

A smart contract is code that is deployed to the blockchain. Each smart contract contains code that can have a predefined set of inputs. Smart contracts can also store data. Following the distributed model of the blockchain, smart contracts run on every node in this technology, and each contract's data is stored in every node. This data can be queried at anytime. Smart contractscan also call other smart contracts, enforce permissions, run workflow logic, perform calculations, etc. Smart contract code is executed within a transaction – so the data stored as a result of running the smart contract (i.e., the state) is part of the blockchain's immutable ledger.

### 50) What do you know about blockchain?

Well, it's a technology which was actually designed for the Bitcoin and later it got a lot of publicity due to the diverse array of benefits it brings when it comes to monitoring and recording all the financial transactions that are made on a network. It's a trusted approach and there are a lot of organizations in the present scenario which are using it. As everything is secure, and because it's an open source approach, it can easily be trusted for the long run.

### 51) How is a block recognized in the Blockchain approach?

Every block in this online ledger basically consists of a hash pointer which acts as a link to the block which is prior to it, transaction data and in fact a stamp of time.

### 52) What are the benefits of Blockchain that you know?

It encourages secure online transactions which is one of its biggest benefits. Basically, being a distributed and decentralized ledger that keeps a close eye on all the transaction records, it doesn't let the record be altered by anyone. This enhances the security. In addition to this, participants and the business owners can always make sure of low-cost auditing at the end. One thing that can always be assured with blockchain is every block or unit can be transferred only once which simply eliminates the double-spending problem.

### 53) What are the two types of records that are present in the blockchain database?

These records are block records and transactional records. Both these records can easily be accessed, and the best thing is it is possible to integrate them with each other without following the complex algorithms.

### 54) What is the principle on which blockchain technology is based?

It enables information to be distributed among the users without being copied.

### 55) Is Blockchain an incorruptible ledger?

As per the developer's claim, the blockchain ledger cannot be corrupted.

### 56) How is a blockchain ledger different from an ordinary one?

The first and in fact the prime difference is Blockchain is a digital ledger that can be decentralized very easily. The chances of error in this approach are far less than in an ordinary ledger. An ordinary ledger is one prepared with hands or by human efforts while the Blockchain performs all its tasks automatically. You just need to configure it in a proper manner and by following all the guidelines.

### 57) What is an Altcoin?

An Altcoin is basically an alternative coin, which are all the cryptocurrencies other than the Bitcoin. This term covers the more than 70 other cryptocurrencies that currently exist in circulation, all fighting to become the next Bitcoin. Just like with the Bitcoin, Altcoins are not regulated by any bank, but instead by the market.

### 58) How long does a deposit take?

Depositing with any cryptocurrency takes from 10 minutes to a little over an hour, depending on which wallet you are using and how fast the transaction can be approved in the server. In rare cases deposits are taking longer, but in general it is very fast. Should you find that a deposit is not credited to your account within a couple of hours, then try and contact the site as there might be some sort of error.

### 59) How long does a withdrawal take?

Withdrawal timeframes depend on the site on which you are withdrawing. The cryptocurrency system will take up to a couple of hours to process the money to your wallet, once the site has sent it, but first the site you are playing on will have to process it. Usually you will receive your money within 24 hours as most sites process cash-outs instantly.

### 60) Is it possible to buy less than 1 coin?

Yes, it is. Since the different coins all have different values, it has been made possible to buy fractions of a coin, fitting the amount of money that you want to spend.

### 61) What is a private key?

A **private key** in the context of Bitcoin is a secret number that allows Bitcoins to be spent. Every Bitcoin wallet contains one or more private keys, which are saved in the wallet file. The private keys are mathematically related to all Bitcoin addresses generated for the wallet. Because the private key is the "ticket" that allows someone to spend Bitcoins, it is important that these are kept secure. Private keys can be kept on computer files, but in some cases are also short enough that they can be printed on paper.

Some wallets allow private keys to be imported without generating any transactions while other wallets or services require that the private key be swept. When a private key is swept, a transaction is broadcast that sends the balance controlled by the private key to a new address in the wallet. Just as with any other transaction, there is risk of swept transactions to be double-spending.

In contrast, Bitcoin provides a facility to import a private key without creating a sweep transaction. This is considered very dangerous, and not intended to be used even by power users or experts except in very specific cases. Bitcoins can be easily stolen at any time, from a wallet which has imported an untrusted or otherwise insecure private key – this can include private keys generated offline and never seen by someone else.

## 62) What are the characteristics of a currency to be aware of?

Although cryptocurrencies are all based on blockchain technology, they are not all created equal. Here are some differences that you need to understand to make informed trading decisions:

- Transaction processing speed
- Total supply currently available
- Will there ultimately be a limit on the total number of currency available?
- Will there be an unlimited supply of currency?
- Is there a real-world need for this software/currency?
- Real world adoption of the technology
- Any big investors in the project?
- Does the use of the software make sense?
- Do the founders have a reputable background?

These are just a few of the characteristics that you should look at. But once you start digging into these details, you will begin to see which projects could work for their intended purpose and which ones are probably scams.

This understanding will also allow you to assess the long-term viability of these different currencies and which ones will be more desirable in the future.

**63) How do I buy Altcoins?**

First buy Bitcoin or Ethereum because those are the coins that are most easily transacted against the smaller Altcoins.

**64) How do I store cryptocurrencies?**

With fiat currency like US dollars, you can store them at the bank or in your wallet. It's pretty straightforward. But with digital currencies, there are a few wrinkles that you need to get your head around, but the idea is similar. Let's take a look at how cryptocurrency storage works.

You store your cryptocurrencies on the blockchain in a "wallet." This is simply an address on the blockchain. It's like how the website address tradingheroes.com directs you to my website on the internet.

**Each wallet has a public address and a private address.** The public address is the address that people send funds to. The private address is the "password" that you use to access and send your funds. Never expose your private key until you are ready to spend your funds, otherwise you will probably lose all the money in your wallet.

Now that you understand the basics of cryptocurrency wallets, let's look at the different wallet options out there. Here are the different ways that you can store your loot:

- **Online wallet:** This is probably the easiest way to store your money. But it is also the least secure. So it's not a good long-term storage solution, but it is fine for buying things and funding your trading accounts. Exchanges like Coinbase also have their own wallets built in.

- **Mobile wallet:** You can download a mobile app like Mycelium to store your spending money. It is more secure than an online wallet, but if your phone ever breaks or gets hacked, everything in your wallet will be gone.

- **Desktop wallet:** Similar to a mobile app but just for desktop computers.

- **Hardware wallet:** These are hardware devices that are built especially for storing cryptocurrency keys. They are safer than the options above, but they are still susceptible to the things that can damage all electronic devices.

- **Paper wallet:** You can also store your private key on paper. This is the most hacker proof, but it is also the least convenient. If you are going to go this route, be sure to store them in a safe place (like a safety deposit box) and don't actually use paper. Use a paper wallet to make sure that your money isn't lost to something as simple as a spilled beer.

## 65) What is the minimum cryptocurrency deposit or withdrawal?

The minimum withdrawal for each transaction is determined by network fee, and the withdrawal sum must be larger than the fee. There is no minimum deposit limit for cryptocurrency operations.

## 66) What is initial coin offering (ICO)?

ICO stands for "initial coin offering" and it is a means of raising capital through a crowdfunding campaign with the use of crypto-assets as investment. A digital asset, the coin or the token, is issued for a purpose and sold to raise money for the said purpose. After the ICO process is done, the coins are traded on crypto-exchanges and market supply and demand decides on their fair pricing.

**67) What is a crypto airdrop?**

A crypto airdrop is when a blockchain project distributes free tokens or coins to the crypto community. To be a recipient of an crypto airdrop often the only requirement is that you have coins from the relevant blockchain stored in your wallet.

# CRYPTO TRADING & INVESTING LESSONS LEARNED OVER THE PAST YEARS

**Courtesy of Chris Dunn**

1. Everyone's a genius in a bull market. Real traders can survive and even thrive in bear markets or highly volatile markets.

2. Don't be a blind bull. ALL markets are cyclical. Don't be afraid of pullbacks or market crashes – that's where you can make the most money.

3. There's a big difference between a trade and an investment.

4. Fully plan your trade before you pull the trigger on the entry.

5. Entries are important, but risk & money management is where you make or lose money.

6. Beware of get-rich-quick gurus hopping on the crypto bandwagon over the past year.

7. Decide which types of trade setups or investments you'll take and ignore everything else.

8. Don't assume just because you've made a lot of money in crypto that you can just as easily make

money in other financial markets. 95%+ of stock market traders LOSE money. The game is rigged. Stick to what you know works for you.

9. The best way to day trade cryptocurrencies is – DON'T!

10. The best way to profit in any market is to find something you think has big potential early (before the general public catches on), and invest assuming you're going to lose 100% of your capital. It's the "angel investor" approach.

11. You can't control the market. The only thing you can control is your entries, trade size, and exits.

12. One market participant can completely destroy "good technical analysis."

13. Don't blindly follow trade alerts from ANYONE, especially random people on social media or chat rooms.

14. All financial networking marketing projects are Ponzi schemes, period.

15. If you make a life-changing amount of money, do NOTHING for at least 30 days.

16. Trading isn't about picking exact tops and bottoms in a market – it's about catching the meat of a move.

17. Don't turn a small losing trade into a massive losing investment.

18. Don't set daily profit target goals – set long-term performance goals.

19. Learn to survive, then thrive.

20. The best charting indicators are price action and volume. You can use others, but it won't necessarily make you a more profitable trader.

21. Trends can go way past what seems rational.

22. Don't try to pick tops in a market. Wait for the market to tell you when the trend is over.

23. Don't trade in front of big news events – it's impossible to predict how markets will react.

24. The biggest challenge for most traders is their ego, or the need to be right.

25. You can lose 50% of your trades and still be profitable if you manage risk properly.

26. The best entrepreneurs and CEOs typically make the worst traders and investors.

27. People with the best mindset for investing typically have a career in high-risk situations like firefighters, pilots, police.

28. Avoid pump and dump groups like the plague they are.

29. You WILL make every mistake in the book. Don't beat yourself up when you make mistakes, just learn and try not to make the same mistake twice.

30. Don't treat crypto exchanges like bank accounts. You don't own the coins unless you control the private keys.

31. Crypto is a 24/7/365 market. You can't catch every trade. If you miss one, don't worry – there's ALWAYS another trade.

# CRYPTO TRADING & INVESTING LESSONS LEARNED

32. Don't invest in a coin unless you understand it inside out.

33. You can make money trading the momentum and hype in shitcoins, just don't invest long-term.

34. Stay away from coins with low trading volume and low market caps. They are easily manipulated and you can get stuck in a position.

35. Don't trade with money you need for living expenses. It's called "risk capital" for a reason.

36. Think of yourself as a hunter – save your ammo for the big game.

37. Cryptocurrency exchanges go down when there's high volatility. If price hits a major target or buy zone, it might make sense to place some orders BEFORE everyone else.

38. Trading and investing brings all your emotions to the forefront – fear, greed, hesitation.

39. The hardest thing to do in trading is... NOTHING. This can also be the most profitable thing to do.

40. Just because a market is in a "bubble" doesn't mean it's going to die. Bitcoin has been through over half a dozen big bubbles and increased in price after each one.

41. Manage your trades in a way that would leave you with no regrets no matter what the market does.

42. Learn to think like a contrarian. If you're someone who needs to have your opinion validated by everyone around you, then trading and investing isn't for you.

43. The shorter the chart time frame, the less reliable the chart patterns are. The longer the time frame, the more variables affect price action and the harder it becomes to predict price. My sweet spot is the daily chart for trade setups and 60-minute chart for entries.

44. Some market conditions are great for pushing the gas on every trade setup you can find, where other market conditions call for you to slam on the brakes and step away from the markets altogether.

45. 90%+ of cryptocurrencies will eventually go to zero. Invest accordingly.

46. The mental side of trading is the hardest to master, the most under-appreciated skill, and will cause you to make or lose the biggest amounts of money.

47. The 3 biggest problems for traders are over-trading, hesitating on entries, and closing positions prior to profit targets when the trade is still intact.

48. You can make a career's worth of profit in one year or one trade – don't feel like every day has to be a home run. Play the long game. Be patient and wait for the best plays.

49. Don't trust anyone else to trade for you. Manage your own high-risk investments (like crypto trading) or don't participate at all.

50. Take the news for what it is – they're trying to get views and clicks. They're NOT looking out for your best interests or trying to help you make money.

# CRYPTOCURRENCY EXCHANGES IN INDIA

- https://www.zebpay.com/
- https://www.unocoin.com/
- https://coinsecure.in/
- https://www.bitxoxo.com
- https://btcxindia.com/
- https://www.buyucoin.com/
- https://www.flitpay.in/
- https://coindelta.com/
- https://coinswitch.co/
- https://pocketbits.in/
- https://coinomi.com/
- https://www.redipay.com/

# ABOUT OUR SERVICES

Similar to Bitcoin, the internet has been one of the greatest gifts that humankind has been given. The Internet has made our lives easy and it has completely changed the way of trade & commerce by creating new opportunities for startups to reach out to the customers on the online platform and create a stronghold. With the increase in popularity of the internet, more and more companies are joining the World Wide Web to reach new generation customers.

But it has also made some services like web hosting, web designing, domain registration and others highly necessary. However, it is not easy for everyone to find a good company offering these services at an affordable price without compromising the quality of the services.

Well, what can you do? You need to just come to https://www.hostcats.com/ to get what you need.

At Hostcats, we consider ourselves to be completely customer oriented thus we always work hard to provide the best to our customers at a reasonable price.

Here are some of our services:

- **Domain Registration:** Domains serve as the address for your website and it is the key to finding you on the internet. At Hostcats, we offer you variety of domain names from .com, .co, .co.in, .net, .org, .club and several others at a reasonable price. Choose the one you need and give your website a proper address.

- **Web Hosting:** Web hosting services are necessary for bringing your website online. The performance and success of your website

www.ingramcontent.com/pod-product-compliance
Lightning Source LLC
Chambersburg PA
CBHW031423210526
45464CB00005B/2023